Drug Abuse In S
A Student Course Manual

Eighth Edition

Mark J. Minelli, Ph.D.
Central Michigan University

Published by
Stipes Publishing L.L.C.
204 West University Avenue
Champaign, Illinois 61820
www.stipes.com

Cover & interior design by Brian K. McElwain – Stipes Publishing L.L.C.

ISBN: 978-1-60904-444-2

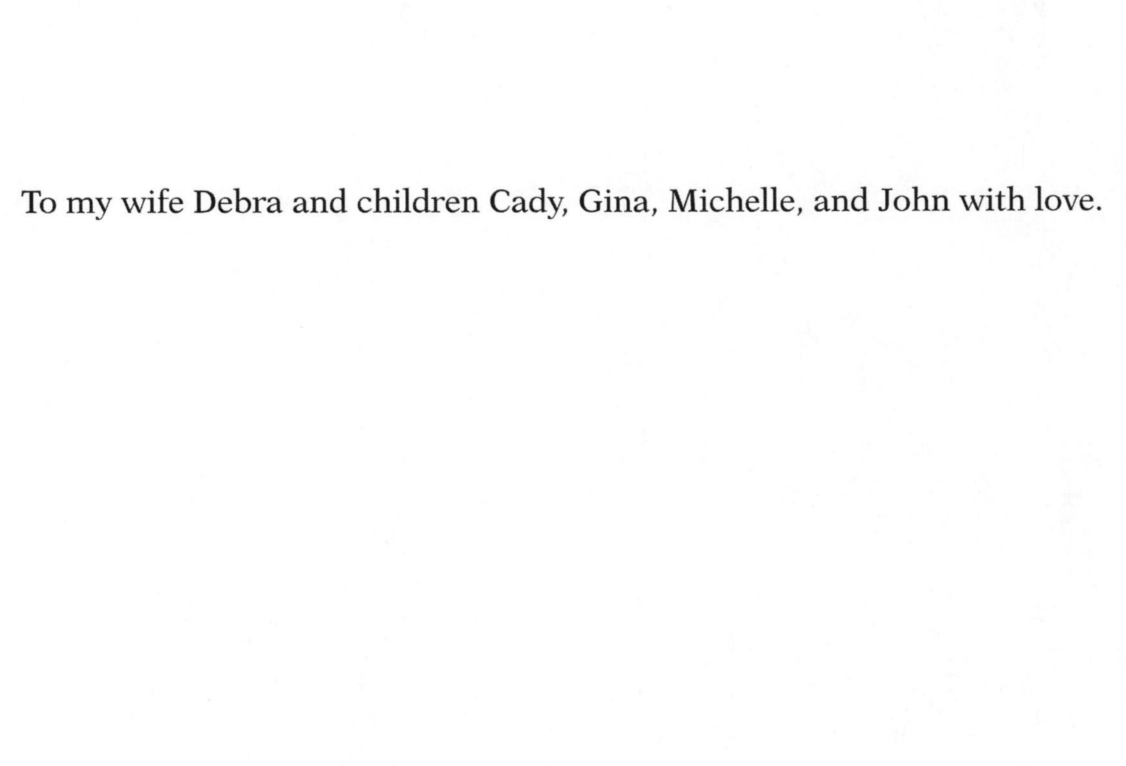

To my wife Debra and children Cady, Gina, Michelle, and John with love.

Table of Contents

Introduction

We reside in a society where drugs surround our existence. As prescription and non-prescription medications have helped to save lives, reduce pain, and enhance the quality of life—we have become a society of drug users and abusers. With the wide variety of chemical substances available to us and societal acceptance of them, it is no wonder that athletes are turning to drugs to improve their performance.

Drug use by student-athletes to improve athletic performance has received much national and international attention. The recent arrests or suspensions of top competitors resulting from drug use has created much publicity in this most important area. Since these events, text books on drugs and athletic performance have surfaced in the marketplace. This manual (in outline format) has been designed with both the student and instructor in mind based on a wide review of scientific literature. Through the author's years of teaching a course on drugs and the athlete, this manual was developed as an outline for a comprehensive discussion of ergogenic aids (performance enhacing drugs, methods, or procedures), or can be developed and used as classroom overhead transparencies and learning activities by the instructor. Further readings to supplement this manual is suggested as the students or intructors search for a deeper understanding of the subject. Ergogenic aids change rapidly—it is also recommended that the users of this manual stay abreast of current press releases, journal articles, and books.

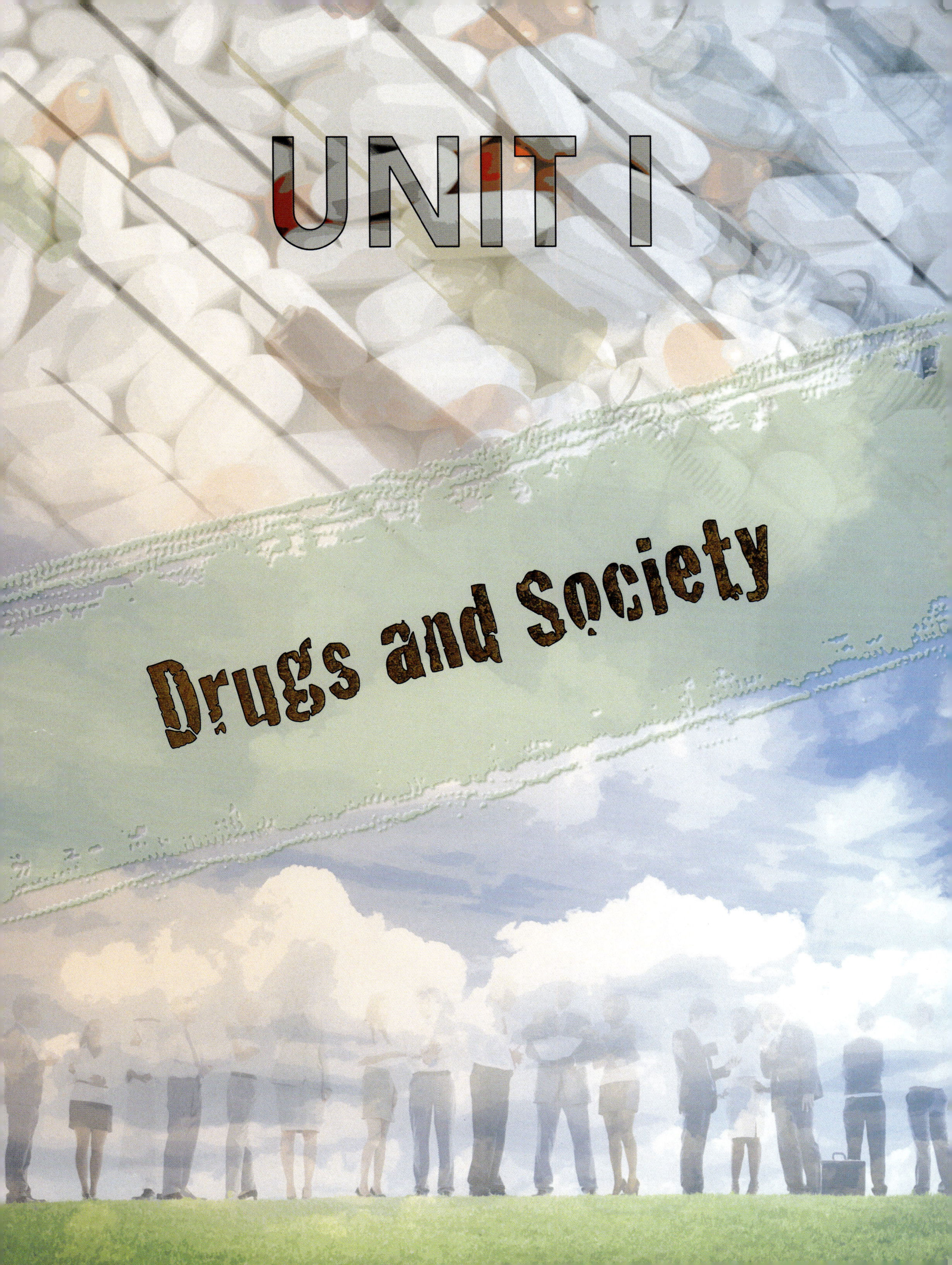

UNIT I

Drugs and Society

UNIT I: Drugs and Society

What is a Drug?

1. A drug is any substance that can produce significant changes in the body, mind, or both.
   A. Chemical name – acetylsalicylic acid
   B. Generic name – aspirin
   C. Brand name – Bayer
2. Drugs have two effects: toxic/therapeutic.
3. All drugs become poisons in high enough doses; some poisons are useful drugs in low doses.
4. Prevention of drug abuse:
   A. Teach people how to satisfy their needs and desires without recourse to drugs.
   B. Teach people how to form good relationships with drugs, to be users and not abusers.
5. Set – what a person expects to happen when they take a drug.
   Setting – the environment in which a person takes a drug (social and cultural).
6. Examples of good relationships with drugs:
   A. Knowledge about the substance and how it effects the body.
   B. Useful effect of the drug.
   C. Ease of separation from use of the chemical.
   D. Freedom from adverse effects on health or behavior.
7. Use to abuse.
   Experimental – nonpattern, short-term, curious, peer pressure
   Use – with groups or friends
   Use (drugs may not be a problem)
   Abuse (drugs may be creating problems)
   Circumstantial – concerts, wedding receptions
   Intensified – daily, relief from problems
   Compulsive

Types of Drugs

1. Endogenous drugs (in the body) from the Greek word – made within.
   A. Endorphins – the brain's own narcotics producing euphoria and reduction of pain.
   B. Uppers – adrenaline, noradrenaline
   C. Downer – serotonin, gaba

(Theory – regular use of a drug from outside the body decreases or shuts down the body's natural chemicals, creating a chemical basis for dependence.)

2. Natural drugs – drugs from plant source which is usually less potent than refined chemicals (coca leaf).
3. Refined drugs – morphine, cocaine, mescaline drugs from plants that come in refined forms.
4. Semisynthetic drugs
   A. This is the transfer of natural drugs into new substances, example – LSD from a fungus called ergot or morphine to heroin.
   B. Usually more potent and toxic.
5. Synthetic drugs
   A. May be the most dangerous of all drugs.
   B. Made from scratch in the laboratory, example – PCP, Valium, Seconal.
   C. Designer drugs – chemically altered drugs forming new drug compounds (i.e. Fentanyl – a synthetic narcotic more potent than morphine – side effects include nausea, decreased blood pressure, vomiting, and possible death from cardiac or respiratory arrest.) (MDMA-Ecstasy – a hallucinogen with amphetamine like properties – side effects include nausea, sleeplessness, depression, jaw clenching, teeth grinding, panic and heatstroke which can lead to collapse and coma.).

Why People Use Drugs

1. To aid in religious practices.
   A. Marijuana – ancient India
   B. Psychedelic plants – Native Americans
   C. Alcohol – Catholic church services
2. To explore self.
3. To alter moods – relieve anxiety, depression, insomnia, boredom, pain.
4. To treat disease.
5. To promote and enhance social interaction – coffee breaks, cocktail hours, business meetings.

Alcohol is a legal, potentially addictive drug.
(Copyright © 2016 Piotr Marcinski)

6. To enhance sensory experience and pleasure.
7. To stimulate artistic creativity and performance.
   A. Edgar Allen Poe – use of opiates
   B. Jazz and Rock musicians
8. To improve physical performance.
   A. Athletes – amphetamines, anabolic-androgenic steroids, cocaine, college athlete self-reported use of ergogenic drugs has decreased since 1989.
   B. Warriors – before battle
   C. Pressure or desire to win (sometimes at any cost).
   D. In search of the competitive edge.
9. To rebel.
10. To go along with peer pressure.
11. To establish an identity.

Drug Addiction

1. Defined as a behavior that exhibits a compulsive need to take drugs.
   A. Behavioral "loss of control" even when experiencing negative consequences.
   B. Drugs act as powerful reinforcers that work on the brain's reward system.
2. All types of drugs: alcohol, amphetamines, cocaine, morphine and nicotine appear to affect neurons in the same part of the brain.
   A. The brain becomes hypersensitive, when drugs are taken as neurons release dopamine. Body movement, emotional response and pleasure are all associated with dopamine.

Alcohol, Tobacco, and Illicit Drug Use in the Past Month Among Persons Aged 12 or Older: Percentages, 2013*

Substance	Past Month
Alcohol	52.2%
Cigarettes	21.3%
Smokeless Tobacco	3.4%
Marijuana	7.5%
Pain Relievers	2.5%
Methamphetamine	0.2%
Cocaine	0.6%
Hallucinogens	0.5%

*Source: SAMHSA, Office of Applied Studies, National Survey on Drug Use & Health, 2013.

Drug Abuse In Sports Recent Historical Timeline

- 1960-International Olympic Committee (IOC) discusses the use of amphetamines-pep pills, scientific research & potential dangers of drugs in sports.
- 1960-Dr. John Ziegler, experiments with anabolic steroids and U.S. weightlifters after discussions with Russian trainers and found success with his athletes.
- 1963-IOC recommends 1. Educate officials & athletes about the dangers of doping. 2. Study behavior of athletes involved in doping. 3. Later established the Medical Commission to study doping in sports.
- 1967-Tour de France cyclist Tommy Simpson dies from amphetamine-related complications.
- 1968-Drug testing begins at Olympic Games in Mexico City but excludes anabolic steroids as reliable tests not established at that time.
- 1976-Anabolic steroids were tested at the Montreal Olympic Games.
- 1981-First person to lose a world record is U.S. discus thrower Ben Plunknett because of steroid use
- 1983-Human growth hormone (HGH) becomes popular as an anabolic steroid substitute and no testing is available to find cheaters.
- 1984-Beta-blockers are now included at the Calgary Winter Games.
- 1985-FDA approves biosynthetic HGH for Genentech Pharmaceutical Company.
- 1986-The National Collegiate Athletic Association (NCAA) develops a drug testing policy after national surveys indicate college athletes are doping in sports.
- 1987-Professional sports begins testing players for anabolic steroids with the National Football league taking the lead.
- 1988-Olympic sprinter Ben Johnson loss a gold medal which brings anabolic steroid abuse into the public's eye.
- 1990's-Other professional sports teams start banning and getting tougher on drug abuse in sports.
- 2000-U.S. Anti-Doping Agency is created.
- 2007-Current-Various sports figures disclosed and penalized of using performance enhancing drugs including Barry Bonds-baseball, Floyd Landis-cyclist, Marion Jones-runner, Alberto Contador-cyclist, Kelli White-runner, Tim Montgomery-runner, Lance Armstrong-cyclist.

UNIT I

Student Activity Worksheet

Name Hollis Kang

Date 10/27/22

Step 1

Make a list of the favorite ten things you like to do.

1. sleeping
2. eating
3. walking my dogs
4. hanging out with friends
5. playing lacrosse
6. watching TV
7. excercising
8. swimming
9. listening to music
10. reading

Step 2

From the list in Step 1, select your top five choices.

1. exercising (–)
2. sleeping (–)
3. playing lacrosse (–)
4. hanging out with friends (–)
5. eating (–)

Step 3

While looking at your top five items, put a "+" sign next to them if alcohol or other drugs enhance that experience or a "-" sign if it detracts from that experience.

Step 4

Do you have more "+" or "-" signs next to your favorite things to do? What does this tell you?

I have all "–" signs next to my favorite things. This tells me that alcohol or other drugs take away from many things, including my favorite things.

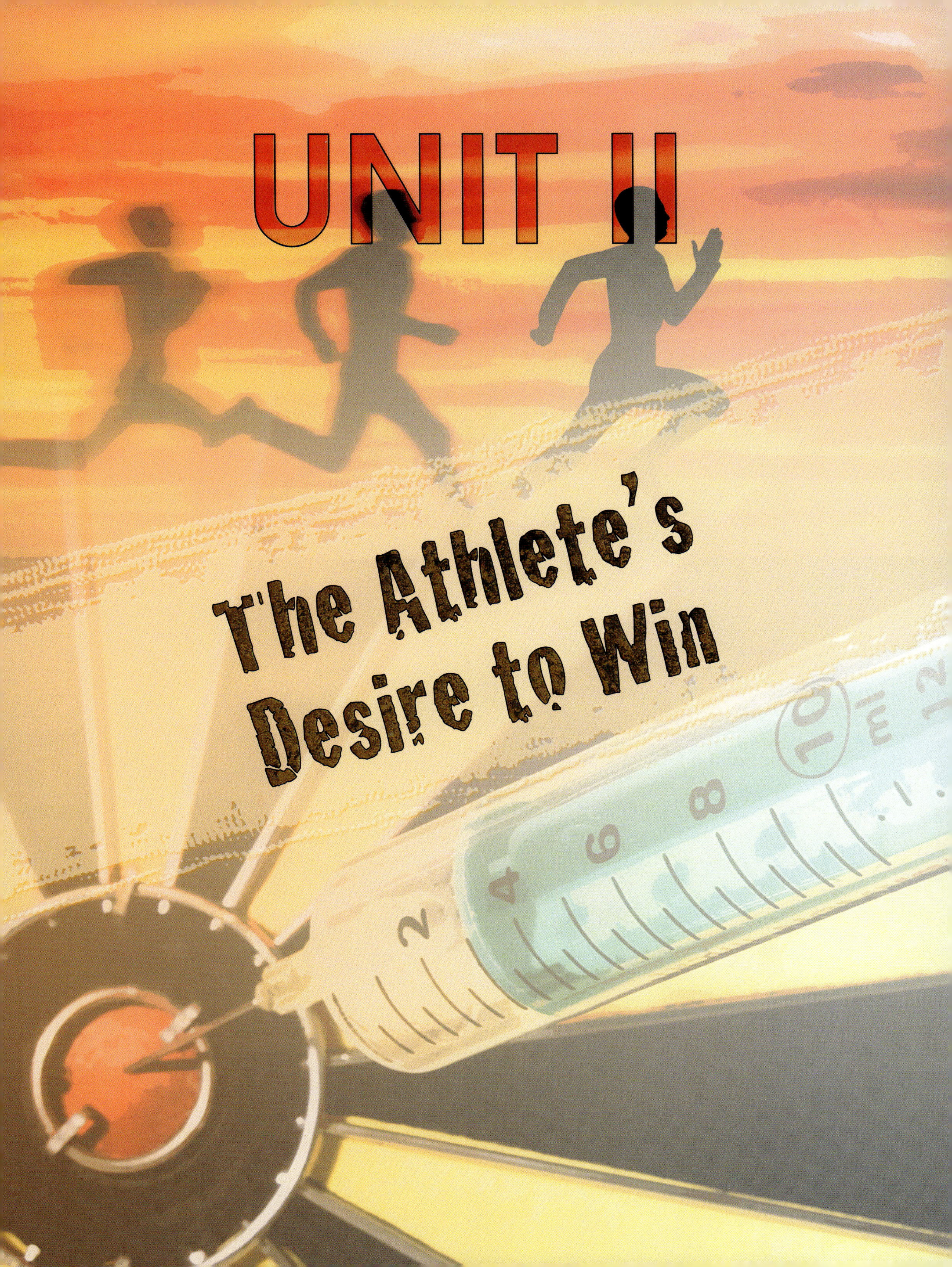
UNIT II
The Athlete's
Desire to Win

UNIT II: The Athlete's Desire to Win

Paradigm of Athletic Preparation and Success

1. All athletic opponents meet on the same field of play (i.e., court, mat, field, rink, gymnasium, etc.)
2. As the athletes abilites improve and mature, the will or desire to win can become increasingly important.
3. Methods of improvement available to athletes:
   A. Skill practice
   B. Progressive weight resistance training
   C. Flexibility exercises
   D. Nutritional dietary habits, supplementation, current scientific information
   E. Equipment and facilities for athletic training
   F. Performance enhancing drugs and methods
   G. Coaching staff experience and training
   H. Sports medicine support personnel experience and training
   I. Relaxation, visualization, concentration, and body awareness exercises and techniques
   J. Personal commitment to their sport and to excellence
   K. Supportive training and personal environment to achieve excellence
   L. Future scientific discoveries in relation to exercise, training, equipment, etc.
   M. High need to achieve
   N. Feedback
      (1) Knowledge of performance
      (2) Knoewledge of results

   (Heredity can also play an important role in body size, shape, etc., which can be an advantage in particular sports and playing positions. An individual is a product of heredity and environment. Performance = skill + motivation.)
4. Regulating bodies and organizations (i.e., National Collegiate Athletic Association, International Olympic Committee, Major League Baseball, etc.) maintain a sphere of influence over athletic competition
5. All of these personal desires, methods, systems, organizations, etc., play a role in athletic competition and the desire to win

External and Internal Pressures Faced by Athletes

1. Having to restrain emotions (except for winning) both in and out of competition
2. Immediate consequences and/or embarrassment for errors made while in competition
3. Denial of physical and emotional pain

4. Fear of failing or not being able to repeat past successful athletic performance and skill level
5. Having to be the best, a winner, number one, etc.
6. Extra time and monetary demands placed on the athlete and their families for training, nutritional plans, equipment, travel, etc.
7. Celebrating success and sometimes leisure time with alcohol "play hard/drink hard" attitude
8. Advertisements during sporting events by major alcohol and tobacco companies (and sponsorship of teams by taverns at the local level)
9. Seeking help is a sign of weakness which can lead to loss of stature in the eyes of teammates, coaches, etc.
10. Curiosity of trying scientifically unproven legal or illegal ergogenic aids or taking performance enhancing drugs to gain a competitive edge
11. Placing too much personal self-worth on being an athlete so when competitive career ends, personal self-esteem is affected

Adapted from: Ted Klontz Lectures, Onsite Training & Consulting, 2455 West Chicago, Rapid City, SD 57702

Ways to Cope With Pressure

Cope – acronym which describes four cognitive and behavioral strategies

(C) Control emotions

(O) Organize input, know the difference between important and unimportant information

(P) Plan response, based on recent feedback and experiences

(E) Execute

Failure can be emotionally devistating to an athlete.
(Copyright © 2016 Ljupco Smokovski)

Qualities of Successful Sports Competitors

1. Risk taking, willing to take risks, action which can lead to bodily harm or failure
2. Stimulus seeking, enjoy challenge
3. Competitiveness
4. Self-confidence
5. Attentional style
6. Expectation for success
7. Cognitive strategies
8. Ability to regulate stress

Psychological Determinants of Drug Use to Potentiate Athletic Success

1. Dichotomous thinking: cognitive distortion that makes anything less than 100 percent unacceptable. An example of this would be an Olympic athlete who feels like a failure after "only" winning the silver medal. Such thinking often compels extreme behavior.
2. Irrational beliefs: I must win. I must be the best. I must never give up. These are a few of the false assumptions that often motivate self destructive behavior. In one form of cognitive therapy, an individual's beliefs are challenged and ultimately reframed as in "it would be nice to win, but no one's perfect."
3. Social phobia: this disabling fear of failing or embarrassing one's self in front of other people usually results in avoiding all forms of public performance. It might also contribute to behaviors that maximize the likelihood of success.

Winning At All Costs

Methods of Improvement Available to Athletes:

- Weight training
- Flexibility exercises
- Nutrition information
- Updated sports equipment
- Performance enhancing drugs
- Training facilities
- Coaching
- Medical support personnel
- Relaxation exercises
- Concentration exercises
- Visualization exercises
- Performance enhancing methods (blood doping, etc.)
- Body awareness tech.
- Commitment to the sport
- Future scientific discoveries
- Heredity
- Environment
- Skill practice
- Feedback
- Counseling services
- Legal performance enhancing aids

Sphere of Influence: NCAA

(Keeping systems in check) **USOC**

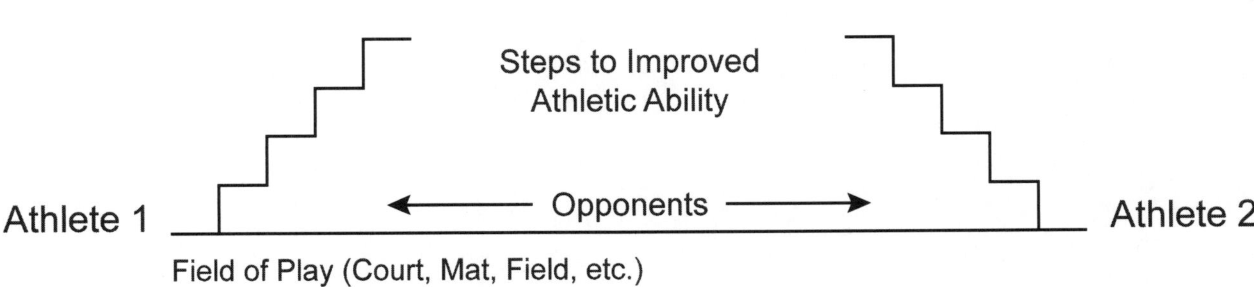

UNIT II

Student Activity Worksheet

Name Hollis Kang

Date 10/27/22

Step 1

From the paradigm described in this unit, list what methods you currently use to train and achieve athletic success..

Skill practice, weight training, flexibility exercises (stretching), equipment and facilities, coaching staff experience and training, relaxation, visualization, etc, personal commitment, supportive training and environment, high need to achieve, and feedback

Step 2

What other methods, training, etc., could you add to improve your current athletic abilites?

I think I could incorporate the nutrition side of it more in order to improve my current athletic abilities. This is something super important because your body needs adequate fuel in order to preform at your highest level. This would include things like having nutritional dietary habits.

Step 3

Do you see any potential problems with your selections in steps 1 and 2?

The only potential problems I see with my selections is that I currently think there are things I could do better. For example, being more attentive to the foods I eat as well as getting enough sleep for how much activity I do.

UNIT III
Alcohol and Alcoholism

UNIT III: Alcohol and Alcoholism

Types of Alcohol

1. Methyl – wood alcohol or methanol
2. Ethylene – used in antifreeze
3. Isopropyl – rubbing alcohol used for medical purposes
4. Ethyl – alcoholic beverages

Alcohol and the Body

1. Nutritional issues
   A. Alcohol abuse can cause a depletion of vitamin B1 (thiamine) which can lead to Wernickes-Korsakoff Syndrome, beri beri, brain damage, and heart trouble.

   Wernicke-Korsakoff Syndrome may exhibit confusion, disorientation, and loss of control over voluntary muscles.

   Beri beri can cause muscle tissue atrophy and swelling of body parts which may lead to over-extension of the heart muscle.

   B. Niacin (vitamin B) depletion.

   C. Vitamin B12 depletion can cause anemia and make one susceptible to bruising.

   D. Poor utilization of vitamin C.

   E. Alcoholic beverages have little or no nutritional value.
2. Brain (progression of intoxication)
   A. Frontal lobe – loss of inhibitions, mild euphoria, impaired judgement, impulsitivity, emotionalism

   B. Midbrain – body movement, coordination, senses

   C. Hindbrain – automatic functions, consciousness
3. Skin – dilation of the capillaries in the face, also provides false sensation of warmth.
4. Water balance – alcohol acts as a diuretic forcing water out of the cells which can produce headaches, dry mouth, and increased urine production.
5. Vision – produces tunnel vision, difficulty in focusing, and blurred or double vision.
6. Muscular system – Alcoholic shaking of the hands, muscle cramps, muscle atrophy making one weak, and less able to perform.
7. Gastrointestinal system
   A. Interferes with digestion, ulcers can develop, irritation and inflammation of the esophagus, stomach, small instestine, and pancreas.

   B. Increased risk of cancer of the tongue, mouth, throat, esophagus, liver, large intestine, and rectum.

8. Liver – acute hepatitis/fatty liver can lead to cirrhosis.
9. Sexual functioning
    A. Men – prostatitis, atrophy of the testicles, decreased sperm production, toxic liver can't break down estrogen causing breast enlargement, loss of body hair, muscle atrophy
    B. Women – loss of libido, loss of menstruation, infertility

Potential Consequences of Alcohol Misuse For College Aged Youth

Blackouts

Hangovers

Drinking and driving violations

Death from overdose

Unplanned and unprotected sex

Date rape

Violence

Missing classes

Lowered academic performance

Behaviors resulting in embarrassment, loss of friendships, etc.

Adverse effects on athletic performance lasting up to 48 hours after use

Theories of Alcoholism

1. Tension Relief and Anxiety Control – individual experiences anxiety, finds relief through drinking which can create additional problems, and further anxiety.
2. Social Learning Theory – positive feelings from drinking, social approval, peer group reinforcement, parents drinking habits, portrays drinking as okay.
3. Psycho-Dynamic Theory – developed by Sigmund Freud and states that the alcoholic is stuck in the oral phase of development, same as smoker, instant gratification.
4. Modeling Theory – family as role model of dysfunctional behavior, alcohol/drug abuse, shame based on family systems.
5. Heredity Theory
    A. Gabrielli's research indicated sons of alcoholic fathers had EEG variations (brain waves) similar to the father but not found in normal population, even after months of sobriety.
    B. You have a 50-50 chance of becoming alcoholic if a parent was/is alcoholic.
    C. Certain neurotransmitters have been identified as possible inherited mechanisms.
    D. An abnormal gene may play a role in predisposing a person to alcoholism (located on chromosome 11 and governs the D2 dopamine receptor of brain neurons).

E. Possible defect in the metabolism of acetaldehyde, which produces addictive substances known as tetrahydroisoquinolines (THIQs).

6. X-Theory – a combination of theories, unknown factors, abusive drinking over a period of years may lead to addiction.
7. Psychological Vulnerability – (sometimes referred to as addictive personality) factors in life that make substance abuse more likely to develop.

Alcoholism as a Disease

1. In 1957, the American Medical Association declared alcoholism to be a disease. The criteria used included the following:
   A. A known etiology (cause).
   B. The symptoms get progressively worse over time.
   C. Outcome factors are predictable.

Current Use Rates

1. Results from the 2010 Nation Survey on Drug Use and Health: summary of national findings indicate that 51.8% of Americans aged 12 or older are current drinkers.
   A. 23.1% participated in binge drinking (defined as having five or more drinks on the same occasion at least 1 day of the past 30 days).
   B. Heavy drinking was reported by 6.7% of the population 12 or older (heavy drinking is defined as binge drinking on at least 5 days in the past 30 days).

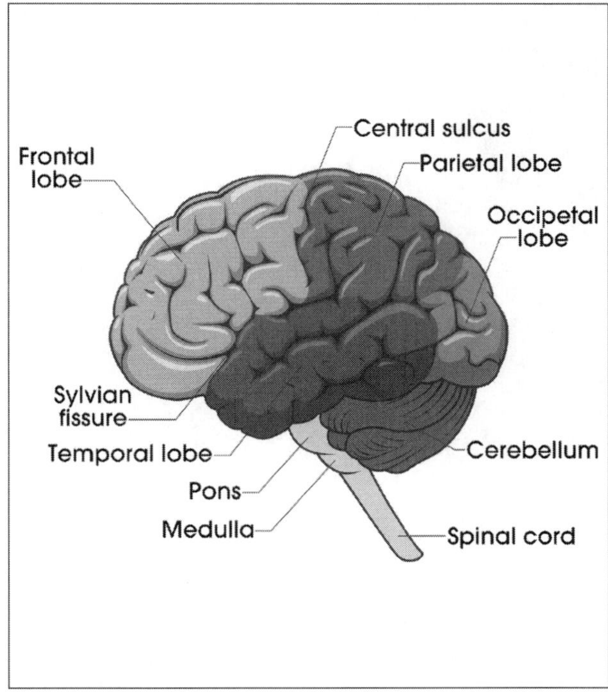

Diagram of human brain.
(Copyright © 2016 Alexander_P)

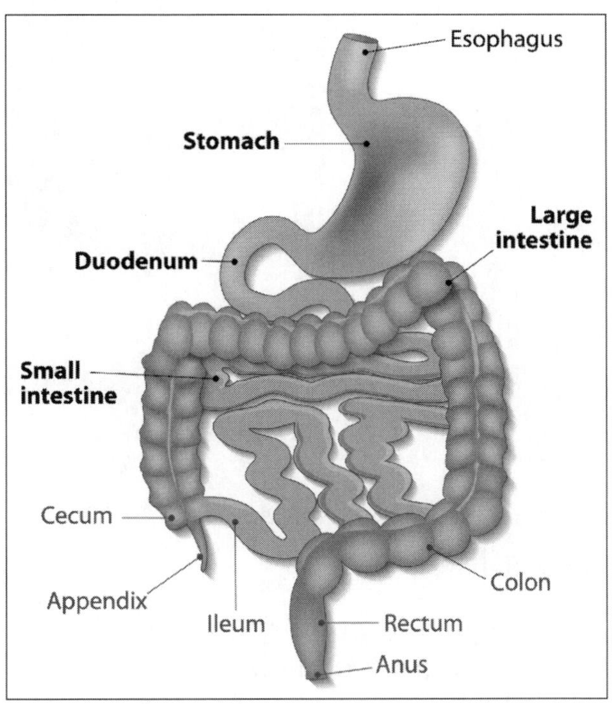

Diagram of gastrointestinal system.
(Copyright © 2016 Designua)

Alcohol Use by College Student-Athletes: NCAA 2013 Survey Results

1. 81% of college student-athletes used alcohol within the last 12 months.
2. 82% of females and 80% of male student-athletes had used alsohol within the past 12 months.
3. 44% of males reported having 5+ drinks at one setting and 33% of female student-athletes reported 4+ drinks in the same time frame (sometimes used to define binge drinking).
4. The survey reported that excessive drinking overall is going down in student-athletes.

Muscular System

A. Ethanol ingestion can have negative consequences for muscle metabolism due to the effects on glucose availability to fuel muscle protein synthesis during recovery from exercise.

B. Studies have shown a decrease in basal protein synthesis by 15 to 20 percent in skeletal muscle after 24 hours of ethanol intoxication.

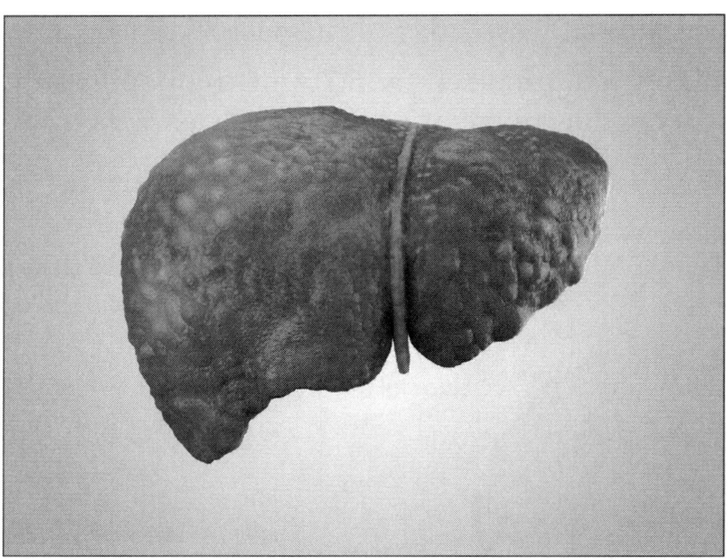

Cirrhosis of the liver.
(Copyright © 2016 eranicle)

Absinthe

1. Originally popular in the U.S. in New Orleans. This green liqueur historically had wormwood oil added, a hallucinogen. This means you had a combination of alcohol and a psychoactive substance.
2. It was often combined with water poured over a sugar cube due to its' poor taste.

3. Brands of absinthe sold in the U.S. today contain very little if any wormwood oil (thujone).

Fetal Alcohol Spectrum Disorders

1. Alcohol can cross the placenta and can interfer with fetal development often called Fetal Alcohol Spectrum Disorders.
   A. It is the known leading cause of mental retardation.
   B. The first trimester of pregnancy the fetus appears to be at higher risk of developing problems which can be physical, behavioral, and/or mental.
   C. It is estimated that 40,000 babies are born each year with this condition.
   D. Physical symptoms can include: head and facial anomalies, smaller brain size at birth, flat cheeks, small head, and thin lips. Other issues may include retarded growth, malformation of various organs, and central nervous system problems.
   E. Behavioral problems can include: short attention span, poor impulse control, hyperactivity, and poor coordination.
   F. Pregnant women are advised not to drink during pregnancy.

Adult Children of Alcoholics (ACOAs)

1. Children raised in homes of an alcoholic parent can have very difficult and stressful lives. Over the years, literature has been devoted to this group with some common findings.
   A. These children find it difficult to receive and give love.
   B. May develop a higher level of responsibility.
   C. Are easily depressed and may devalue themselves.
   D. Have fear of abandonment and handle authority poorly.
   E. Need to feel in control of their environment.

Alcohols Strain On Society

1. A wide variety of problems are associated with the abuse of alcohol in our society and include:
   A. Motor vehicle accidents – the leading cause of death in ages 15 to 20
   B. Other accidents – falls, burns, drownings, workplace accidents, sports related accidents
   C. Suicide – a majority of suicide attempts are alcohol related and appears to be more related to people who commit suicide impulsively and premeditated suicide.
   D. Domestic violence issues
   E. Date rape – alcohol is still considered the number one date rape drug.
   F. Criminal related activities – breaking and entering, drunk driving, minors in possession, assault, etc.

UNIT III

Student Activity Worksheet

Name____

Date____

Step 1

Describe how alcohol use or non-use is viewed by your family or cultural ethnic background.

Step 2

What types of ceremonies, customs, etc., involve alcohol? How or why is alcohol used for these events?

Step 3

How is drunkenness viewed by your family or cultural ethnic background?

Step 4

Explain or provide examples of how you can make friends without the use of alcohol.

UNIT IV

Tobacco

UNIT IV: Tobacco

Cigarettes in America

1. Brought to America by tourists visiting England, men smoked cigars, women smoked cigarettes.
2. During the Civil War cigarettes were part of the military ration because of their smaller size.
3. Between 1895 and 1921, 14 states banned cigarettes.
4. During World War I cigarettes were part of every soldier's ration, smoking increased. This happened again in World War II.
5. In 1939 the first scientific study linking lung cancer to cigarette smoking was published.
6. During the 1950s cigarette smoking was linked to lung cancer and heart disease, yet the number of smokers increased.
7. In 1966 the Cigarette Labeling and Advertising Act required a health warning on cigarette packages.
8. During 1967 the tobacco industry spent $250 million on advertising and was the single biggest advertiser on television.
9. In 1971 Congress banned all cigarette advertising on radio and television.
10. The American Medical Association called for no advertising at all and a smoke free society by the year 2000.

    A. Smoking remains the number one preventable cause of death in this country.
11. Results from the 2013 National Survey on Drug Use and Health: Summary of National Findings indicate that during the past month 25.5% of those 12 or older were current users of tobacco products. In addition, 21.3% were current cigarette smokers, 4.7% smoked cigars, 3.4% used smokeless tobacco, and 0.9% smoked tobacco in pipes.

Hazardous Components of Cigarette Smoke

1. There are more than 3,000 components of tobacco smoke. Two of the more common gases are carbon monoxide and hydrogen cyanide.

Carbon Monoxide (CO)

1. This poisonous component is a colorless, odorless gas and makes up 1 to 5% of the smoke in an average cigarette.
2. Carbon monoxide displaces oxygen in the blood and muscles need oxygen to carry off waste products.
3. Problems result in circulation damage, edema, cholesterol deposits, increased diseases of the respiratory system, sudden death from coronary heart disease, and fetal damage.

Hydrogen Cyanide and Nitrogen Oxide

1. Effects lining of the respiratory airways, chronic obstructive pulmonary disease, and emphysema.
2. The inhaling smoker retains 70% of the particulates they breathe.

Tars

1. Of the known cancer causing agents or carcinogens in cigarette smoke, tar is composed of the thousands of chemicals in cigarette smoke that condenses to form a sticky residue in the lungs.

Nicotine

1. Nicotine contains an alkaloid poison which is the addictive element in tobacco. Studies have shown that smokers injected with nicotine had no desire to smoke.
2. This drug acts on the adrenal glands to release stimulants called catecholamines. This raises blood pressure and heart rate.
3. With regular use, levels of nicotine accumulate in the body during the day and persist overnight. Thus, daily tobacco users are exposed to the effects nicotine for 24 hours each day.

Effects of Smoking on Health

1. Smoking is attributed to nearly 480,000 early deaths each year from cancers and diseases of the lung, heart, and circulatory system.
2. Coronary heart disease is the single most cause of mortality among cigarette smokers. Smokers have twice the risk of this as nonsmokers. After about ten years the risk of coronary heart disease in ex-smokers approaches that of non-smokers.
3. Smokers, on the average, die 10 years earlier than nonsmokers.

Cancer

1. One out of every five cancer deaths is smoking related.
2. Smoking is linked to cancer of the larynx, pharynx, oral cavity, esophagus, pancreas, and bladder.
3. Lung cancer risk is ten times higher in smokers.
4. There is a 400% increase in women's lung cancer in the last 30 years.

Respiratory Disease

1. Cigarette smoking is the most important cause of chronic obstructive pulmonary disease, chronic bronchitis, and emphysema.
2. Smoke inhibits the ciliary motion responsible for cleansing the respiratory tract.
3. Smokers have more respiratory infections and miss more work days than their nonsmoking counterparts.

Pipe and Cigar Smoke

1. Cigar sales have increased 50% between 1993-1997. Increases are mainly in occasional cigar smoking by young middle-aged men of higher economic status. Use has also increased in teens and women.
2. Regular cigar smoking increase the risk of coronary heart disease, chronic obstructive pulmonary disease, cancer of the digestive tract and lung.

Other Effects

1. Cigarette smokers require greater doses of pain-killing and anxiety reducing drugs to be effective.
2. Smoking effects the body's ability to utilize vitamin C.
3. Women smokers who use oral contraceptives greatly increase their risk of heart attacks.
4. Nicotine slightly improves short-term memory and concentration, but declines 4 hours after the last cigarette.

Right of the Nonsmokers

1. Sidestream smoke can irritate the eyes, nose, and throat. This smoke often has higher concentrations of irritating and hazardous substances than does mainstream smoke.
2. The Center for Disease Control states that sidestream smoke is blamed for 3,800 lung cancer deaths yearly and 8,000 to 26,000 asthma cases in children.
3. A meta-analysis of 18 studies dealing with the dangers of secondhand smoke concludes that a nonsmoker's risk of heart disease can increase by 25% with exposure to secondhand smoke.

Maternal Smoking

1. During the last two trimesters of pregnancy if the mother smokes she may experience babies of lowered birth weight, increased risks of stillbirth, spontaneous abortion, premature birth, and neonatal death.
2. Carbon monoxide passes across the placenta reducing fetal oxygen, fetal growth is retarded due to this lack of oxygen supply.
3. Lowers the levels of vitamin C in breast milk.
4. If the mother stops smoking by the fourth month of pregnancy, there appears to be no increased risk to the fetus.

Smoking Cessation Programs

1. Over 40 million people have quit smoking. Most do this on their own and some through a formal program.
2. Men are more successful than women.

3. Methods:

   Cold turkey

   Acupuncture

   Hypnosis

   Support groups or buddy system

   Nicotine patch – the nicotine patch adheres to your skin and releases nicotine into your bloodstream. There are different strenghts of patches. Some come in different levels of nicotine and are usually worn on the skin for 16 to 24 hours a day. Side affects include skin redness, burning and itching, along with nightmares (if patch is worn throughout the night).

   Nicotine gum – this product is chewed briefly to release nicotine and then rests in your mouth. The released nicotine is absorbed into the blood through your mouth and gums. Gum user experience fewer withdrawal symptoms and cravings for nicotine as the dosage is reduced until they are completely weaned. Nicotine gum can cause headache, nausea, upset stomach, and dizziness.

   Nicotine nasal spray – nicotine spray allows you to spray small doses of nicotine into your nasal passages, reducing your urge for nicotine. This form of therapy is available through your doctor. Side effects include nasal irritation at onset of usage, runny nose, throat irritation, watering eyes, sneezing, and cough.

   Zyban – the first nicotine-free medicine designed to help smokers quit and is available only through a doctor. You start taking the medication and continue to smoke until you reach a quit day, within 1 to 2 weeks after starting treatment with Zyban. It takes about a week for Zyban to reach the right levels in your body to be effective. The most common side effects with Zyban include dry mouth and difficulty sleeping.

   Programs that combine several approaches have shown the most promise.

Smokeless Tobacco (Athletes Tobacco)

1. These products include both chewing tobacco and snuff, which are mixtures of tobacco leaves, various sweeteners, flavorings, and scents.
   A. Chewing tobacco – leaves are shredded, pressed into bricks, cakes, or dried and twisted into rope-like strands.
   B. Snuff – powdered or finely cut tobacco leaves.
   C. Both products are placed in the cheek or between the lower lip and gum.
2. Carcinogenic compounds include polonium-210, aromatic hydrocarbons, and nitrosamines. Strongest link is to cancers of the oral cavity (mouth).
3. The health problems which are commonly associated with the use of smokeless tobacco include: bad breath, abrasion of teeth, gum recession, periodontal bone loss, tooth loss, leukoplakia, nicotine dependency, hypercholesterolemia, hypertension, and various forms of oral cancer.
4. Use rates in a recent NCAA survey for collegiate student-athletes was 17%.
5. The National Collegiate Athletic Association (NCAA) has banned the use of tobacco (including smokeless) by players, coaches, and officials during practices and games.

Potential Steps of Destruction

1. Gingivitis – inflammation of the gums, tissue bleeds upon pressure, treatment is fairly simple and effective at this point.
2. Pyorrhea (pus flowing) – gum tissue separates from the tooth, resulting in possible loss of teeth. Treatment at this stage becomes difficult because the gum tissue does not regrow.
3. Leukoplakia (white patch) – precancerous lesions anywhere on the mucous membrane, mouth, or tongue. One study showed oral leukoplakia was present in 46% of smokeless tobacco users.

Chewing tobacco and chewing tobacco pouches.
(Copyright © 2016 bildfokus.se)

Antique snuff jar.
(Copyright © 2016 Taborsky)

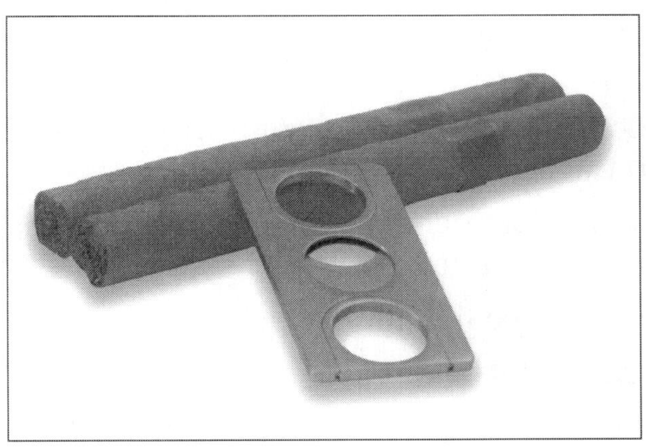

Cigars and cigar cutter.
(Copyright © 2016 Birgit Reitz-Hofmann)

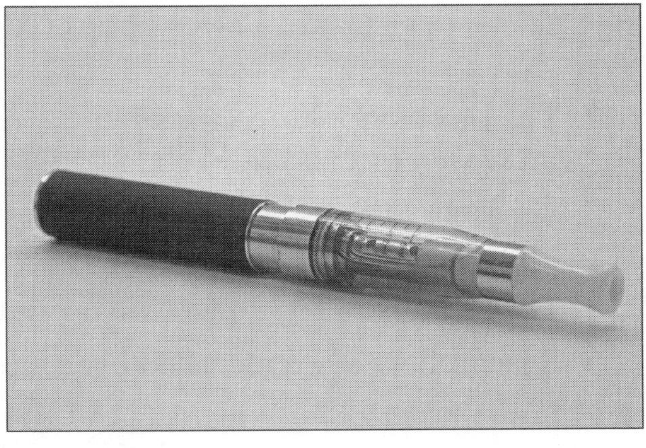

An e-cigarette.
(Copyright © 2016 Enriscapes)

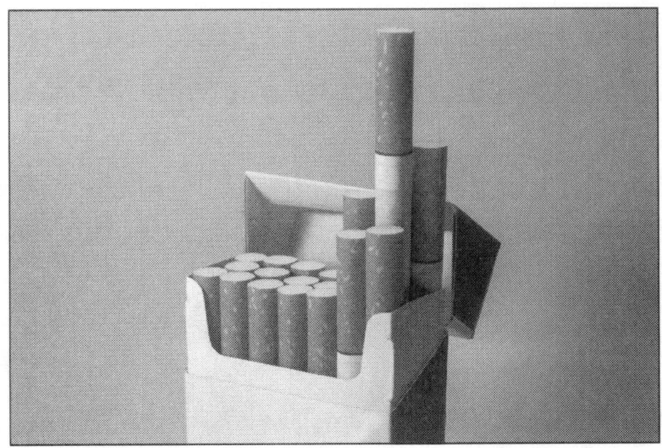

A pack of cigarettes.
(Copyright © 2016 Karel Pesorna)

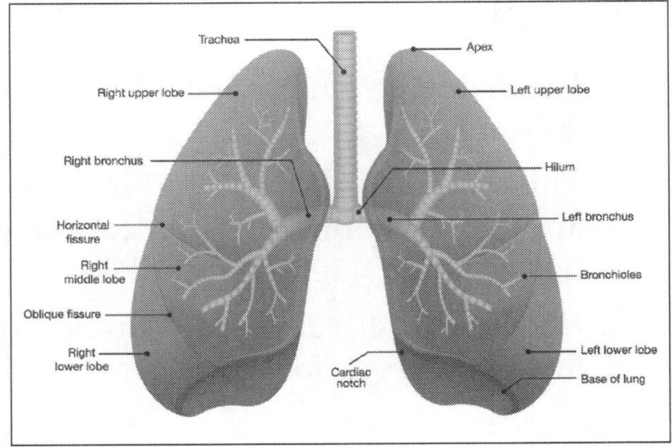

Diagram of human lungs.
(Copyright © 2016 solar22)

A hookah.
(Copyright © 2016 phototrx)

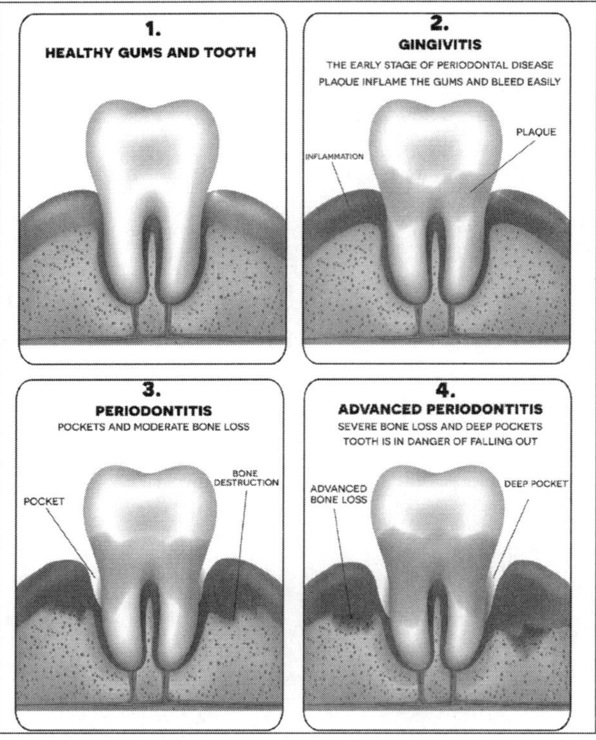

Diagram of gum loss.
(Copyright © 2016 Tefi)

E-Cigarettes

1. These devices are battery powered and turn liquid that contains nicotine into vapor.
2. The more popular e-cigarettes have become, calls to poison control centers have increased due to liquids inside these products affecting young children.
3. Aerosols released from e-cigarettes contain some chemicals (benzene and cadmium) that have been identified as causing cancer and birth defects.
4. This is considered a nicotine product and can be habit forming.
5. Researchers are concerned over the ultrafine particles in e-cigarette vapor.
6. Some research linking e-cigarettes to later use of tobacco products by teenagers.
7. Marketed as a safer alternative to cigarettes or to help people quit smoking.

Hookah Smoking

1. Is considered water-pipe tobacco smoking which has roots from Middle Eastern cultures.
2. This practice is becoming more popular with college students as hookah cafes are being established near college campuses. It may be perceived as being less harmful than cigarette smoking.
3. Negative health effects are similar to cigarette smoking including the risk of heart disease and cancer.
4. Concerns from health professionals arise from both the smoking of tobacco and carcinogens derived from the coal heating of tobacco.

UNIT IV

Student Activity Worksheet

Name____

Date____

Step 1

In your opinion, what percentage of college level student-athletes use smokeless tobacco in each of the following sports:

Baseball________________________________

Football________________________________

Tennis_________________________________

Swimming_______________________________

Women's Softball___________________________

Women's Gymnastics_________________________

Women's Basketball__________________________

Men's Basketball___________________________

Wrestling________________________________

Men's Track & Field__________________________

Women's Track & Field________________________

Step 2

Which sport did you say had the highest use of smokeless tobacco and why?

UNIT V
Marijuana/Hemp

UNIT V: Marijuana/Hemp

Marijuana

1. Second most widely used mind altering substance in this country following only alcohol. Ten million Americans use marijuana each month.
2. At one time, the hemp plant was used for military and commercial purposes in the manufacture of rope.
3. Marijuana is a difficult drug to classify as it started out classified as a narcotic and now it is classified as a hallucinogen.
4. Potency of the plant:

   Street marijuana 8% to 16% THC

   Sinsemilla (buds and tops of female plants) 7.5% to 24% THC

   Hashish (resin from female plants) 2% to 20% THC

   Hash oil (tar-like distilled liquid) 15% to 70% THC
5. Numerous states in America have approved use of medical marijuana and some recreational use.

The Plant

1. Cannabis sativa grows wild or can be cultivated.
2. Active chemicals are delta-9-tetrahydro-cannabinol (THC) and cannabidiol (CBD). It contains 500 known chemicals and when smoked or cooked, these break down into over 2,000 chemicals entering the body. Sixty one of these chemicals are unique and are called cannabinoids.
3. Flowering tops contain the highest THC levels, leaves lesser amounts, stems very little.

Pharmacology

1. The half life of THC is 28-56 hours. Cannabinoids are lipophilic (fat loving) and seek out fatty cells of the body. It takes one month for a single joint to clear from the body or about three months for a chronic smoker.
2. THC increases the heart rate, dilates blood vessels, although tolerance and withdrawal symptoms do not develop, psychological addiction has been noted.
3. Marijuana and tobacco contain roughly equal amounts of irritants and toxic gases. Pot smoke has carcinogens in amounts 50 to 70 percent greater than in tobacco smoke.
4. Chronic bronchitis and more frequent chest colds has been noted with effects similar to smoking tobacco.
5. THC causes relaxation, drowsiness, increased appetite, thirst, and euphoria. Large doses can cause delusions and hallucinations.
6. Impairment of immediate recall has been reported.

7. The amotivational syndrome has not been proven in chronic users, but has been observed by therapists counseling marijuana users.

Marijuana/Hemp Use and Abuse Potential

Potential Uses

1. Marijuana/hemp seeds can be used to produce fuel oil for cooking and protein.
2. Medicinal uses can include treatment for asthma, glaucoma, control of nausea related to cancer chemotherapy, muscle spasms and back pain, stress reduction, appetite stimulant, HIV/AIDS, and sleep aid.
3. Textiles, fabrics, rope, and twine.
4. Paper products including money, books, newspaper, etc.
5. Paints and varnishes.
6. Help fight erosion as the plant has deep roots.

Potential Abuses

1. Impairs coordination making it hazardous to drive a car, operate heavy machinery, fly a plane, etc.
2. Causes mild anxiety or panic reactions in some users.
3. Irritates lung tissue, causes decreased pulmonary function when smoked, and contains carcinogens.
4. Causes tachycardia similar to mild stress.
5. Increases potential to have babies of lower birth weight (less than five pounds, withdrawal syndrome has also been observed in newborns).
6. Dependency or inability to quit or reduce usage of the drug.
7. Impairs memory and learning abilities.
8. Reduction in motivation/productivity (amotivational syndrome).
9. Reduces testosterone level, sperm count, and libido. Can impair the sperm's ability to fertilize the egg.

From left to right: marijuana buds and trimmings; budding marijuana plants.

Ergogenic Effects

1. Although marijuana is not a performance enhancing drug, athletes may use this substance to reduce the feelings of stress and anxiety prior to or after competition. Some athletes may use marijuana for relaxation and as a sleep aid. The idea that adequate sleep can improve performance.
2. The use of cannabis has shown in research studies that it can impair exercise performance, psychomotor (slower reaction times, sedation), and cognition.

UNIT V

Student Activity Worksheet

Name____

Date____

Step 1

From reviewing the potential use and abuse of marijuana/hemp, do you feel marijuana/hemp should be legalized, decriminalized, laws remain the same, or for medical use only? Explain your answer.

UNIT VI

Stimulants/Uppers

UNIT VI: Stimulants/Uppers

Stimulants

1. Stimulants excite the nervous system and make people feel more alert and energetic. They work by causing nerve fibers to release noradrenaline and other stimulating neurotransmitters.
2. Increases heart rate, blood pressure, changes in blood flow to the extremities.
3. Stimulates sympathetic nervous system – fight or flight syndrome. Noradrenaline, like adrenaline, produced by the adrenal glands readies the body for emergencies.
4. Suppresses hunger, sometimes used in diet pills, preparation of the body for emergencies, all digestive functions become non-essential.

Side Effects Include

1. Anxious, jittery, unable to sit still, disrupts sleep patterns, heart palpitations, diarrhea, urinary frequency (immediate post-consumption).
2. Stimulants force the body to give up its own energy reserves. Wears off less energy than usual "down" sleepiness, lethargy, mental fatigue, and depression (post-high).

Common Stimulants

1. Caffeine
2. Cocaine
3. Amphetamines
4. Look-alike drugs
5. Nicotine
6. Over-the-counter drugs
7. Energy drinks

Caffeine

1. The average coffee drinker consumes 1,000 cups per year.
2. Soft drinks are where kids get their caffeine.
3. Caffeine is the most popular natural stimulant.
4. Caffeine levels in food and drinks is not regulated by the U.S. Food and Drug Administration. A popular ingredient in energy drinks.

Side Effects Include

1. Nervousness, anxiety, irritability, muscle twitching, jitteriness, and insomnia.

2. Caffeine is the possible cause of fibrocystic breast disease (benign breast lumps), cancer of the bladder, pancreatitis, and gastrointestinal tract irritation.
3. Cardiovascular disease and birth defects have been linked to excessive use of caffeine.
4. The drug is mildly addictive and increases when combined with sugar.
5. Severe headaches during caffeine withdrawal are common.
6. Coffee is irritating to stomach and bladder. Tea is not as irritating to the body.
7. It has been suggested that an intake of 500 to 600 mg (milligrams) of caffeine per day (approximately 4 to 7 cups of coffee) represents a significant health risk.
   A. A study of 39,000 Norwegian men and women who drank five or more cups of coffee daily indicated that the risks of dying from heart disease was considerably above that for persons who drink less or do not consume.
8. Peak concentrations of caffeine are reached at approximately 60 minutes regardless of dose.
9. Half-life of caffeine ranges from 2 to 10 hours depending on the research study. There is virtually no caffeine in the human body 24 hours after administration.
10. Alcohol combined with high-energy drinks can be a dangerous combination leading to rapid heartbeat and nausea.
11. The caffeine content in energy drinks is similar to a cup of coffee.

Lower Risk

Youngsters – 1 or 2 sodas per day

Adults – 1 to 4 cups of coffee or tea per day

Energy Drinks

1. Primarily supplies caffeine, a stimulant drug for shorterm energy boost.
2. Most energy drinks contain about the same caffeine level as a cup of coffee.
3. When the effects wear off fatigue sets in. Can also speed the rate of fluid loss.

Ergogenic Effects

1. The benefits on performance appear to be associated with general perception of well being, increased alertness, increased endurance, carbohydrate sparing, and enhanced skeletal muscle contractile properties. Endurance performance improvements have been clearly demonstrated by the use of caffeine.
2. Caffeine in combination with carbohydrate can result in increased muscle glycogen resynthesis.

Caffeine Contents of Various Products*	
Product	**Caffeine (mg)**
Coffee (8 ounce cup):	
Drip method	115-175
Brewed	80-135
Instant	65-100
Decaffeinated	2-5
Tea (8 ounce cup):	
Brewed	40-60
Instant tea	30
Iced tea	47
Cocoa (1 ounce):	
Milk chocolate	6
Baking chocolate	35
Soft Drinks (12 ounces):	
Mountain Dew	55.0
Mello-Yello	52.0
Tab	46.0
Coca-Cola	34.0
Diet Coke	46.0
Dr. Pepper	41.0
Pepsi Cola	37.5
Diet Pepsi	36.0
Jolt	71.0
Red Bull (8.2 ounces)	80.0
Stimulants:	
No-Doz tablets	100
Vivarin	200

*Data for caffeine content obtained from Consumers Union, Food and Drug Administration, National Coffee Association, National Soft Drink Association, Bunker and McWilliams, Pepsi, Slim-Fast, and Physicians Desk Reference for Non-Prescription Drugs, http://www.math.utah.edu/~yp/ee/fun/caffeine.html.

Cocaine

1. Coca leaves – erythroxylon coca
   A. Peru and Bolivia – Indians chewed the coca leaves for stamina to work.
   B. Used for anti-fatigue, anti-hunger, and anti-pain, not for a high. Leaves contain about one percent cocaine.
2. Sigmund Freud used it to cure morphine and alcohol habits. Used minimally in medicine as an anesthetic, replaced by procaine and novocaine.

3. Used to be in Coca-Cola until 1930's, replaced with caffeine.

Pharmacology

1. Mucous membranes of the nose – the favored site of use.
2. Local anesthetic action is due to the blockage of the transmission of painful stimuli.
3. Powerful constrictor of small blood vessels. Causes ulceration of the nasal septum.
4. Tolerance and withdrawal occurs in high doses, causes true addiction. Due to high cost people sell possessions, turn to crime, etc.
5. Overdoses produce tremors, convulsions, temporal lobe seizure pattern, and delirium. Death is due either to cardiovascular collapse or respiratory failure.

Cocaine State

1. Causes hyperstimulation, over alertness, euphoria, and feelings of great power.
2. Very short acting (15 minutes to half-hour).
3. Prolonged use can cause depression which promotes using the drug again.
4. Cocaine delays ejaculation and orgasm, sometimes used as an aphrodisiac.

Patterns of Use

1. Street cocaine adulterated with lactose, procaine, amphetamine, or strychnine.
2. Speedball – mixture of cocaine and heroin, carries a high risk of dependency and overdose.

Amphetamines

1. Synthetic stimulants invented in the 1930's with a chemical structure similar to adrenaline and noradrenaline, single dose usually lasts four hours.
2. Amphetamines are more toxic than cocaine when abused as the body can eliminate cocaine faster.
3. World War II soldiers received amphetamines to march longer and fight better. Have been used medically to reduce weight and fight depression.
4. Common amphetamines:
   A. Amphetamine – Benzedrine
   B. Dextroamphetamine – Dexedrine
   C. Methamphetamine – Methedrine
   D. Ritalin – A similar compound
   E. Designer amphetamines: Methcathinone (CAT); MDMA (Ecstasy); Methylenedioxamphetamine (MDA)

5. Today amphetamines are prescribed for only a few conditions.
6. Speed freaks of the 1960's injected the drug. The crash or coming down caused paranoid and psychotic reactions. The new speed freaks are methamphetamine abusers.
7. High use groups:

   College students – to study for exams

   Truckers – long distance travel

   Athletes, actors, and dancers – improve performance
8. Methamphetamines have become increasingly popular with young people due to the low cost and high that can last up to 14 hours. Adverse effects are similar to other stimulants and can increase the CNS of the body to dangerous levels. Violent behavior, paranoia, auditory hallucinations, and even death can occur from methamphetamines.
9. Ice, sometimes called crystal meth and crank, is a powerful methamphetamine and can be smoked or injected. The effects can last 12 hours or more and has shown to reduce resistant to illness and may cause liver, kidney, and lung damage.
10. Methamphetamine labs have become popular, but pose many environmental hazards. Explosions, fires, toxic fumes, and chemical burns can happen and conditions of a meth lab are considered child endangerment. Some mobile meth labs have even been found by police in motor vehicles.

Adderall Abuse

1. Historically it was caffeine, ritalin, and now adderall as the stimulant of students to enhance academic performance. They can stay up for long hours of study and may help them become more focused and organized.
2. A study conducted at the University of Wisconsin at Madison showed one in five college students use adderall and ritalin nonmedically.
3. Adderall is a CNS stimulant used to treat hyperactivity and narcolepsy.
4. Abuse can cause dependency, death, or serious effects on the heart.
5. Get medical help if signs of allergic reaction, hives, difficulty breathing, swelling of your face, lips, tongue, or throat. Other issues include fast, pounding, or uneven heartbeats, feeling light-headed, fainting, severe headache, chest pain, blurred vision, tremors, or hallucinations.

Bath Salts

1. Synthetic powder sold legally online and through drug paraphernalia stores.
2. Common names – ivory wave, purple wave, red dove, scarface.
3. They contain various amphetamine like chemicals including mephedrone and methylone (similar to the drugs found in ecstasy).
4. Can be taken orally, inhalation, and by injection.

5. As with other stimulants there is a high potential of abuse, addiction, and overdose is not uncommon.
6. Signs of overdose include chest pains, increased blood pressure, increased heart rate, agitation, hallucinations, paranoia, and delusions.

Look-Alike Drugs (Amphetamines)

1. Look-alike pharmaceutical amphetamines contain no controlled substances. Dangerous to people with heart disease, high blood pressure, diabetes, or thyroid disease.
2. Available over the counter, head shops, and mail order.
3. Contain caffeine, ephedrine, or phenylpropanolamine either singly or in combination.
   A. Ephedrine occurs in a desert shrub used to treat asthma. Resembles adrenaline, produces more anxiety and less euphoria than amphetamines.
   B. Phenylpropanolamine is a nasal decongestant and is found in many diet pills. Also in cold remedies to offset the drowsiness of antihistamines. They do decrease appetite, and if used over a long period of time can cause dependency.

Cocaine, spoon, and syringe.
(Copyright © 2016 Evdokimov Maxim)

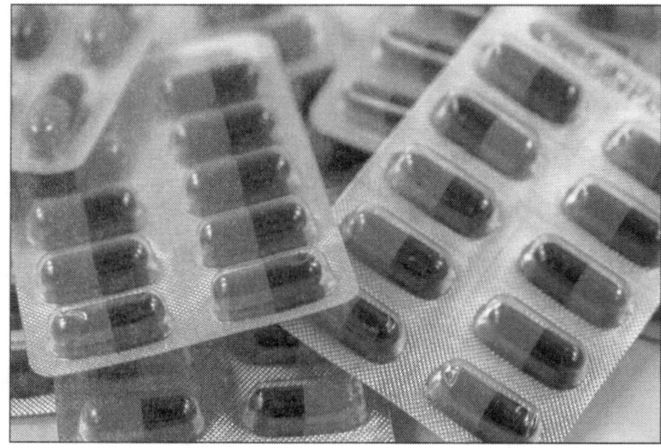

Amphetamines.
(Copyright © 2016 odd-add)

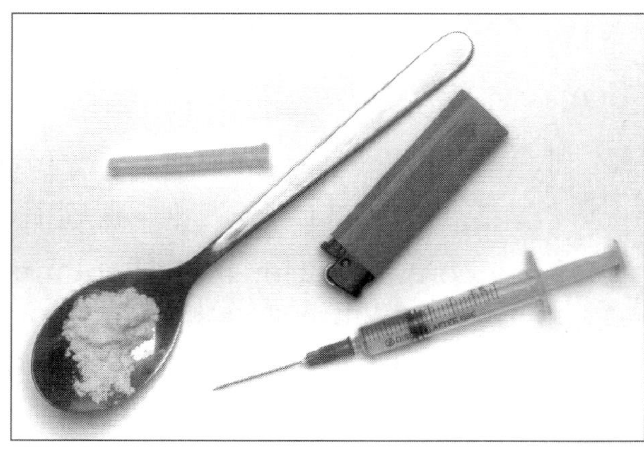

Methamphetamine, spoon, lighter, and syringe.
(Copyright © 2016 ArtTim).

UNIT VI

Student Activity Worksheet

Name____

Date____

Step 1

Make a list of what products you use on a daily or weekly basis that contain stimulants. If taken on a daily basis, are they taken approximately the same time each day?

Step 2

Do you feel you are "hooked" or addicted to any of the items listed in Step 1? Explain your answer.

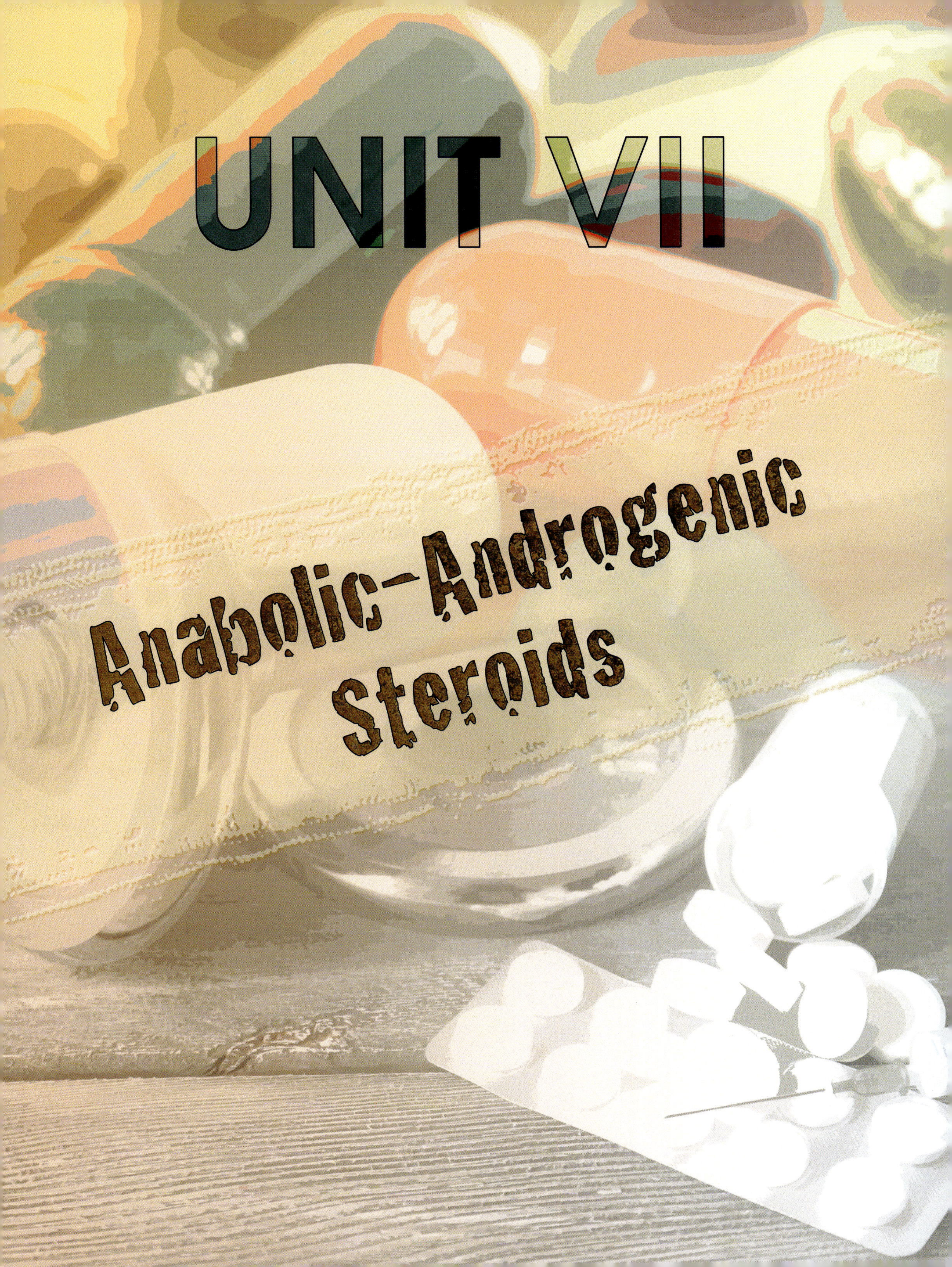
UNIT VII
Anabolic-Androgenic
Steroids

UNIT VII: Anabolic-Androgenic Steroids

Anabolic-Androgenic Steroids

1. Male testosterone – has two functions: 1. development and maintenance of the male secondary sex characteristics (facial hair, deep voice, distribution and amount of body fat). This is the androgenic function of testosterone; 2. anabolic function is the creation of larger muscles.
2. Anabolic androgenic steroids are synthetically derived compounds which mimic the anabolic effects of testosterone and minimize the androgenic effects.
   - A. Steroids – involve the synthesis of protein for muscle growth
   - B. Anabolism – building up process
   - C. Catabolism – breaking down process

Side Effects Include

1. Liver function alteration – toxic hepatitis and tumors.
2. Cardiovascular system impairment – blood clotting disrupted, atherosclerosis, cholesterol increase (LDL), decrease in HDL (good cholesterol), these are considered most hazardous of all side effects reported.
3. Hypertension – high blood pressure.
4. Reproductive process alterations – testicular atrophy and sperm count reduction, triggering of stimulating prostate tumors.
5. Increased aggressiveness – very common sometimes called "roid rage," contributes to harder workouts while on the drug.
6. Development of breast tissue in males – "gynecomastia" increased tissue under the nipple, becomes less prominent, but does not disappear entirely upon discontinuance of the drug, nodules need to be surgically removed.
7. Virilizing effects:
   - A. Males – growth of seminal vesicals, penis, and prostate, thickening of vocal chords, increased body hair, oily skin, increased sexual drive, puffy look, and veins show under skin.
   - B. Females – clitoral enlargement, interrupted or irregular mentrual flow, increased body hair, male pattern baldness, deep voice. Although menstruation returns to normal after discontinuance of the drug, other side effects do not!
8. Various problems – weight loss and strength (usually after the cycle), joint soreness, susceptible to infection, acne, closure of the growth plates (young males). The use of shared needles for the injection of anabolic-androgenic steroids is associated with the transmission of disease such as hepatitis B and HIV/AIDS.
9. Stacking – using oral and injectable steroids together, some studies found that athletes took 4 to 8 times the recommended dose, this potentiates side effects.

10. Micro-tears tendons – torn tendons, muscles too large.
11. Cancers – tumors liver, skin, etc.
12. Psychological depression – weight gain then loss.
13. Rates of usage:
    A. High school level students – males 6.6%; females 0.5%.
    B. Intercollegiate level – current NCAA survey shows 1.4%.
    C. Professional football – no hard data, but some have stated as high as 75%.
14. Psychological dependence – can be caused by positive results of steroid use and increased reinforcement from peers.
15. Muscle dysmorphia – a type of absessive-compulsive disorder. The subject is preoccupied with muscularity, nutrition, dietary supplements, and excessive exercise.

Beneficial Effects From Steroids

1. Therapeutic uses – combat anemia, formulation of bone matrix, improve appetite, promote healing after surgery, weight gain for nutritional deficiencies.
2. Increased strength and muscle size – can increase cellular fluid (sarcoplasm) and general edema (water retention). Heavy training and adequate nutrition should be present.
3. Increased respiratory rate and endurance – cortisol (a stress hormone) levels are increased.
4. Improved recovery time after injury or training – steroids promote synthesis and/or retard nitrogen excretion.

Reason Why People Use Steroids For Ergogenic Effects

1. Researchers have identified three classifications of individuals who may use anabolic-androgenic steroids:
    A. Athletes to enhance performance; seeking increased strength, speed, power, size, and aggressiveness.
    B. Bodybuilders and models for improved body image or physical appearance.
    C. Gang members, police officers, soldiers, etc., to help enhance their fighting skills or level of aggressiveness.

Alternatives to Steroids

1. Supplementation of amino acids, vitamins, minerals, and other nutrients are important along with appropriate training techniques, this will provide lasting improved performance and gains.

Common Anabolic Steroids

1. Oral anabolic-androgenic steroids

Signs and Symptoms of Anabolic-Androgenic Steroid Abuse in Males Progression Chart*

Early Phase

The athlete may:

- See others using steroids and become curious.
- Start to read articles about the dangers and benefits of using steroids and talk to current users.
- Acquire steroids from the black market, medical community, etc.
- Experiment with first steroid cycle.
- Experience weight gain chiefly through retention of water in the cells.
- Feel more aggressive during workouts, recuperate from workouts quicker, have a general feeling of well-being.
- Experience a mild strenght increase (possibly due to placebo effect of drugs), general gain in body mass, or increased aggressiveness.
- Have elevated blood pressure due either to the drugs or increases in weight resistance training.
- Experience an increase in sexual drive resulting from increased use of testosterone derivatives.
- Experience some acne due to oily skin.
- Notice decreases in weight and strength and mild depression upon finishing the steroid cycle.

Middle Phase (potential symptoms of early phase plus new one)

The athlete may:

- Have an urge for increased steroid use (may involve the athlete's self-concept through his appearance.)
- Not be satisfied with normal gains and start a second steroid cycle.
- Feel he is able to work out more often and greater intensity.
- Find his friends changing because he's seeking out other steroid users.
- Increase steroid dosage level or frequency of administration.
- May use both oral and injectable steroids for potential maximum benefits (stacking).
- Notice acne problems resurfacing that may be more extreme than the initial outbreak.
- Experience hair loss.
- Exhibit personality changes interferring with interpersonal relationships.
- Complain of insomnia.
- Exhibit aggessiveness when using, and depression when coming off of steroids.
- Continue cycling of steroids.
- Exhibit azoospermia, the absence of sperm in the semen. (This usually takes 6 to 8 months of steroid use.) May complain of problems of impotence to a physician. May notice frequent or uncontrolled erections.
- Exhibit extreme temper outbursts, aggressive behavior, and general irritability, sometimes called "roid rage."
- Have lowered high-density lipoprotein levels. (These aid the body in removing cholesterol.)

Late Phase (potential symptoms of previous phases plus new ones)

The athlete may:

- Exhibit prostate enlargement.
- Have accelerated atherosclerosis which leads to coronary artery disease (heart attack, stroke, etc.).
- Have liver disease (tumors, peliosis, hepatitis).
- Notice purple or red colored spots on his body.
- Have various cancers (liver, kidney, etc.).
- Notice unnatural hair growth.

The final choices of an athlete out of control with steroid use appear to be:

- To become drug free.
- To continue to have serious health problems, possibly including death.

*From: Minelli, MJ, Thompson, PA, Rapaport, RJ. "Anabolic-Androgenic Steroid Use-Abuse (in Males) Progression Chart." *Addiction & Recovery*, September/October, (1991): 14-16.

A. anadrol (oxymetholone)
B. Anavar (oxandrolone)
C. Dianabol (methandrostenolone)
D. Maxibolin (ethylestrenol)
E. Methyltestosterone
F. Primobolan (methenolone)
G. Proviron (mesterolone)
H. Winstrol (stanozolol)

2. Injectable anabolic-androgenic steroids
   A. Anatrofin (stenobolone)
   B. Bolfortan (testosterone nicotinate)
   C. Deca-Durabolin (nandrolone decanoate)
   D. Delatestryl (testosterone enanthate)
   E. Depo-Testosterone (testosterone cypionate)
   F. Dianabol (methandrostenolone)
   G. Durabolin (nandrolone phenpropionate)
   H. Enoltestovis (hexoxymestrolum)
   I. Equipoise (boldenone-veterinary)
   J. Primobolan (methenolone enanthate).
   K. Sustanon 250 (a mixture of testosterone esters)
   L. Therobolin
   M. Trophobolene
   N. Wintrol V (stenozolol-veterinary)

Corticosteroids

1. These drugs are used as an anti-inflammatroy agent to help relieve pain, and can assist in returning an injured athlete to competition more quickly. They are also used in ophthalmological lotions and dermatologic purposes.
2. Side effects include:
   A. Retard wound healing
   B. Promotes infections
   C. Osteoporosis
   D. Glucose intolerance
   E. Hypertension
   F. Psychological changes

G. Cataracts

H. Pancreatitis

I. Growth inhibition

3. Ergogenic effects:

A. Although this drug can reduce swelling quickly, it may help mask a severe injury causing more damage if the athlete continues to play.

Amino Acids

Building blocks of which proteins are constructed.

1. Twenty are necessary for human growth and metabolism, some are supplied by food, other are produced by the body.
2. Ones provided by food are called essential.
3. Complete proteins – contain all essential amino acids (milk, cheese, eggs, and meat).
4. Incomplete proteins – do not contain all essential amino acids (vegetables, grains).

Human Growth Hormone (HGH)

1. Secreted by the pituitary gland, important for childhood growth. Used for growth deficient children.
2. Stimuli for release of HGH include low blood sugar, sleep, stress, amino acids, and exercise.
3. HGH promotes protein synthesis and nitrogen retention similar to anabolic-androgenic steroids.

A. Retention of too much nitrogen may be a problem if you are not normally deficient.

B. Insulin is the other major anabolic hormone, promotes intracellular transportation of glucose for energy, stimulates protein synthesis, and suppresses protein breakdown.

4. Excessive HGH can cause serious hormonal imbalances and side effects can include:

A. Acromegaly – grotesque facial features.

B. Swelling of the hand and feet.

C. Headaches, mood changes.

D. Visual disturbances.

E. Excessive sweating.

F. Offensive body odor.

G. Diabetes.

H. Death.

I. High blood pressure.

J. Elevated cholesteral and sugar levels.

5. New synthetic form can cost approximately $8,000 to $15,000 per year for injections. Old form was from human pituitary glands caused viral infections and death.
6. Some studies have shown that high levels of HGH can increase mortality levels.

Ergogenic Effects

1. Promotes increases in lean body mass and is very difficult to test for at present.
2. May also preserve skin, boost immunity, improve heart and kidney function when used as an anti-aging hormone.
3. Anti-aging usage – can cause side effects, long term effects are unknown, expensive to use. Studies indicate no data to support anti-aging and life-extending claims.

Gamma-Hydroxybutyrate (GHB)

1. Appears to stimulate the release of human growth hormone (HGH), some bodybuilders are replacing steroids with this and is also used in weight reduction due to its fat burning properties.
2. Overdose can lead to coma and death.
3. FDA pulled GHB off the market as it was listed as a nutritional supplement.
4. Sometimes referred to as "liquid X," GHB may be taking the place of rohypnol as the "date-rape drug." Easily made GHB quickly depresses the respiratory system, especially when mixed with alcohol, which can cause unconsciousness and loss of memory.
5. Side effecrts include:
   A. Low doses can cause agitation and amnesia.
   B. Moderate dosages may cause drowsiness, dizziness, and euphoria.
   C. Higher dosages can cause severe respiratory problems, including breathing difficulty, breathing cessation, nausea, vomiting, seisures, coma, and death.
6. Similar supplements considered dangerous, and sometimes used as date rape drugs, include gamma butyrolactone (GBL) and 1,4 butanediaol (BD).

Tetrahydrogestrinone (THG)

1. Designer steroid derived from chemical modifications of the synthetic steroids trenbolone and gestrinone.
2. Banned by the FDA, appears to be used by track and field athletes along with baseball players.
3. Very limited data on the safety of designer steroids.

Drugs and How Long They Linger

1. Following the drug name is the approximated length of time residues of the drug are detectable in urine, although that varies widely, depending on body weight, metabolism, and drug dosage.

A. Amphetamines: 48 hours
B. Caffeine: 24 hours
C. Barbiturates: short-acting, such as Secobarbital, 24 hours; long-acting, such as Phenobarbital, 2 to 3 weeks
D. Benzodiazepine (including Valium, Librium, Dalmane): 3 days
E. Cocaine: 2 to 4 days
F. Methadone: 3 days
G. Opiates (including Heroin, Morphine, and Codeine): 2 days
H. Propoxyphene (Darvon): 6 to 48 hours
I. THC (Marijuana and Hashish): 6 to 8 weeks for chronic smokers, up to 7 days for a one-time smoker
J. Methaqualone (Quaaludes): 2 weeks
K. Phencyclidine (TCP and PCP): 8 days
L. Anabolic-Androgenic steroids: orals – Dianabol long/dose: 4 days; injectable – Deca-Durabolin 25mg/dose: 50 days

Primary Methods for Community/School-Based Steroid Use Reduction Education and Information*

Methods for Information Dissemination	Location of Educational Interventions
A. Mass media – use of TV talk shows, radio and television public service announcments, newspaper articles, etc. B. Community forums – using knowledgeable professional speakers, peer educators, or individuals recovering from steroid use related problems. C. Printed materials – includes posters, flyers, pamphlets, and brochures on steroid abuse which can be utilized at various locations. D. School-based education – information should be incorporated in health/physical education classes starting at the junior high level and continuing through the collegiate years.	A. Schools – information posted in school locker rooms, health classes, bulletin boards, etc. B. Sporting events – information should be available at football stadium, track and field events, swimming pools, weight gyms, and fitness clubs. C. Pharmacies, hospitals, health facilities – pharmacists, medical doctors, and other health professionals should receive (and make available) updated information about the abuse of steroids in sports.

*This table is reprinted with permission from the *Journal of Physical Education, Recreation & Dance*, October, 1992, 68-74. JOPERD is a publication of The American Alliance for Health, Physical Education, Recreation and Dance, 1900 Association Drive, Reston, VA, 22091.

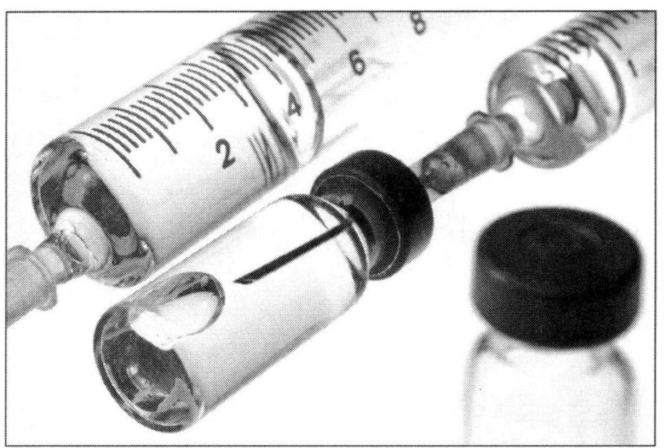

Liquid form of anabolic steroid and syringes.
(Copyright © 2016 Nixx Photography)

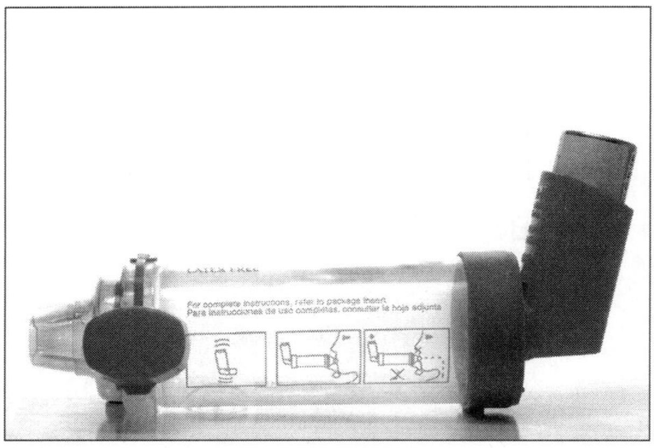

Corticosteroid inhaler tube.
(Copyright © 2016 Rob Byron)

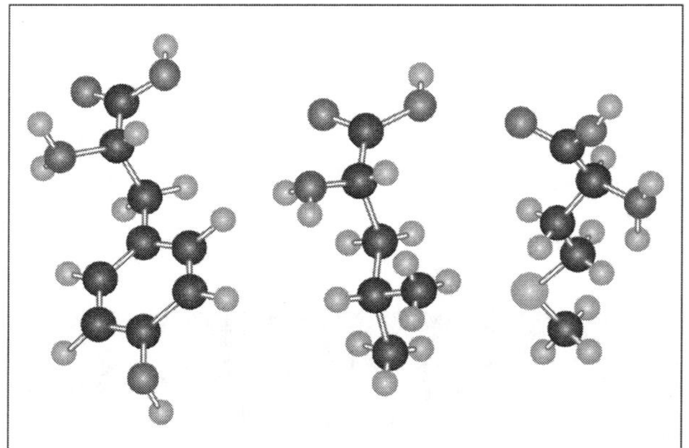

Amino acid molecules (left to right): tyrosine, leucine, and methionine.
(Copyright © 2016 Shmitt Maria)

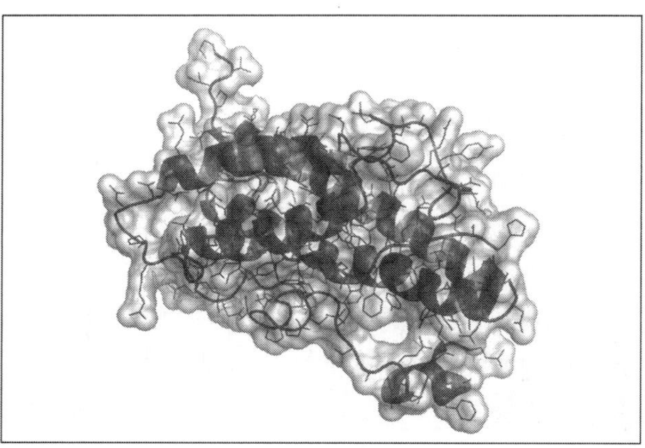

Chemical structure of human growth hormone (HGH).
(Copyright © 2016 molekuul_be)

UNIT VII

Student Activity Worksheet

Name______________________________

Date______________________________

Step 1

If you could take or have access to a drug or sport supplement that would enhance your performance, but may cause a variety of health problems, would you take it?

Yes No

Step 2

Explain your answer in Step 1.

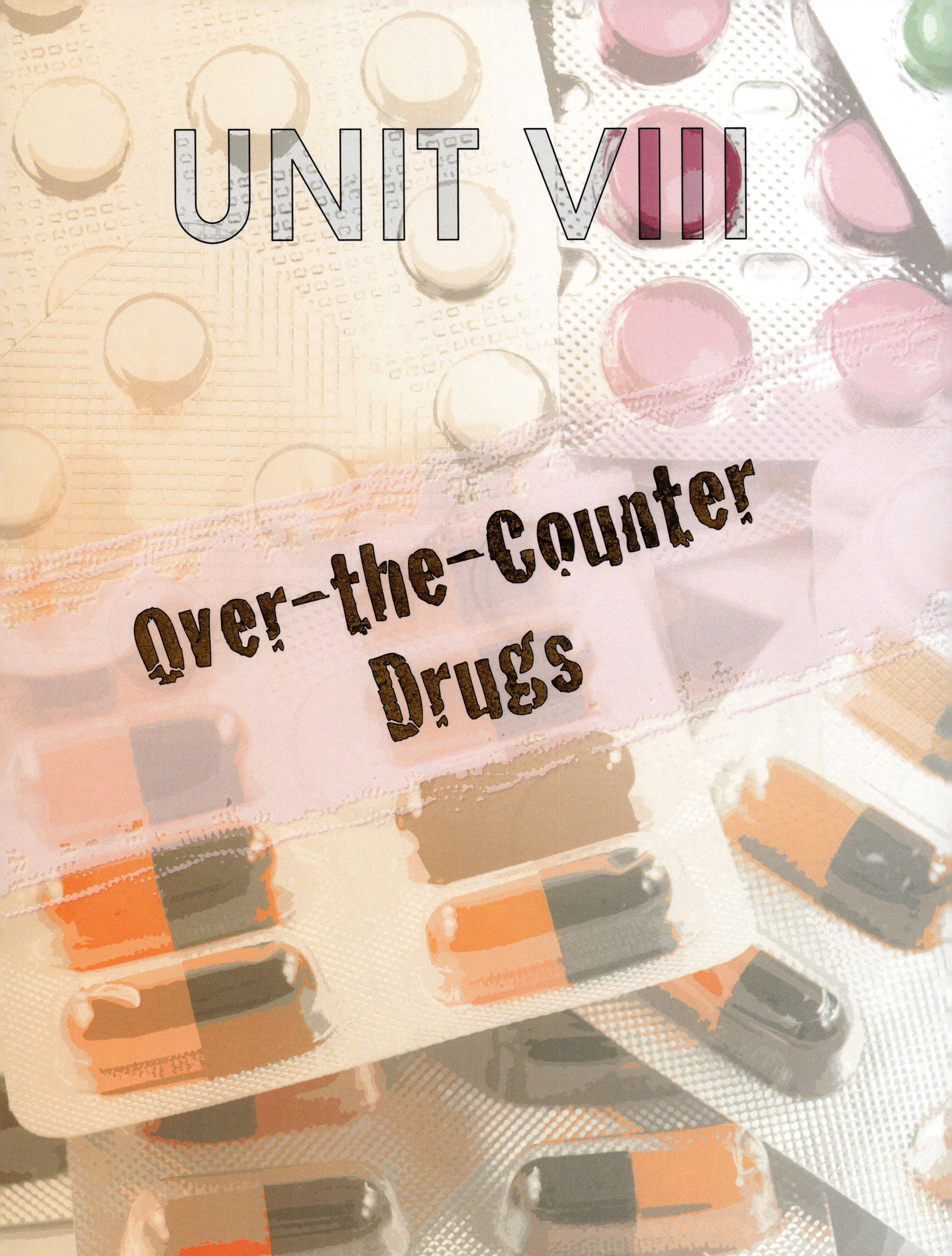
UNIT VIII
Over-the-Counter Drugs

UNIT VIII: Over-the-Counter Drugs

Cold, Cough, and Allergy Drugs (OTC)

1. Americans spend a billion dollars annually on these drugs. They cannot cure the common cold, but can relieve some of the symptoms.
2. Single versus combination products – majority of products contain two or more active ingredients. FDA feels single ingredient products are safer. Single drug for a specific symptom.
3. Time-release products – takes one or two hours after use to reach maximal levels and lasts up to six hours.
4. Advantages (of time-release products):
   A. Easier to take since fewer doses are necessary.
   B. Longer acting relief.
   C. Fewer and less severe side effects because blood levels are fairly constant.
5. Disadvantages – hard to manufacture uniformly effective time-released products.
6. As OTC drugs are legal, athletes, as well as non-athletes, have easy access.

Cough Suppressors

1. A cough's main purpose is to clear the airway. It is a protective physiological reflex part voluntary, part involuntary.
2. Coughing is one way the body fights illness, not always good to suppress with drugs.
3. Drugs work in one of two ways: 1. Act in the brain to depress the cough center; 2. Act on the throat and bronchial passages.
4. Codeine products (narcotic) are considered safe and effective. They should not be used for more than one week.

Allergy

1. Allergic reactions – inflamed nasal membranes, running nose, itchiness in nose and eyes, coughing, shortness of breath, and coma.
2. Individual becomes hypersensitive to the allergen and body secretes histamine, antihistamines counteract these effects by blocking histamine receptor sites on these cells.

Antihistamines

1. Have a mild drying effect.
2. Not really effective for cold symptoms.
3. May cause drowsiness, sometimes used as sleep aids (newer products eliminate drowsiness effects).
4. Should not be used with alcohol or other sedative drugs
5. Should avoid driving a vehicle or operating machinery.

Nasal Decongestants

1. Will relieve nasal stuffiness and improve breathing from colds, hay fever, and allergies.
2. The dry up nasal discharge and constrict swollen blood vessels in the nose and sinuses.
3. Rebound effect – when the drug werars off the blood vessels may swell up more than before. Should use no more than three days in a row.
4. Come in topical applicaton (nose sprays and drops), inhalation (inhales or steam vapors), oral (liquid or tablets).
5. For topical application only one person should use each drug dispenser, in order to prevent the spread of germs.

Aspirin

1. Used to reduce pain, fever, and inflammation.
2. Aspirin products are often used in treating arthritis and preventing heart attacks, strokes, and cataracts.
3. Side effects include:
   A. Stomach irritation
   B. Nausea
   C. Vomiting
   D. Potential overdose
   E. Reye's Syndrome
   F. Allergic reactions
   G. Dizziness
   H. Diarrhea
   I. Mask injury, return to competition too soon.

Acetaminophen

1. Used to reduce pain and fever.
2. Acetaminophen products are often used in place of aspirin due to fewer reported side effects.
3. Side effects include:
   A. Nausea
   B. Vomiting
   C. Upset stomach
   D. Long term use may cause liver damage.
   E. Hepatitis
   F. Reduced white blood cell and platelet count.

G. Allergic reactions have been reported but are rare.
H. Mask injury, return to competition too soon.

Ibuprofen

1. Can be used to reduce pain, fever, and inflammation.
2. Often used to replace aspirin products as ibuprofen has fewer side effects and has been found to be effective in relief of mentrual cramps.
3. Side effects include:
   A. Similar to aspirin products.
   B. Sensitivity to sunlight.
   C. Kidney damage.
   D. Gastrointestinal bleeding.
   E. Allergic reactions.
   F. Mask injury, return to competition too soon.

Naproxen Sodium

1. Used to reduce fever, muscle pain, arthritis, menstrual pain, and lessen inflammation.
2. Fewer side effects than other analgesics and is long lasting.
3. It is not advised to use alcohol when taking this drug.
4. Side effects include:
   A. Stomach upset.
   B. Gastrointestinal bleeding.
   C. Bloating.
   D. Dizziness.

Antihistamines: nasal spray, prescription cough syrup, eye drops, and capsules.

Pseudoephedrine

1. This OTC drug is known as Sudafed. The drug is metabolized in the body to Cathine, a banned substance.
2. Athletes have used this drug in high doses to provide an ergogenic effect. Studies have conflicting results on this but most show no performance enhancing effects.
3. This nasal decongestant is used to relieve symptoms of the common cold, hay fever, or other upper respiratory allergies.

UNIT VIII

Student Activity Worksheet

Name____

Date____

Step 1

Find the price of these over the counter drugs at your local pharmacy or discount store.

	Brand Name Price	Generic/Company Version Price
Aspirin		
Acetaminophen		
Nasal decongestant		

Step 2

What did you learn from doing this consumer research study?

UNIT IX
Nutrition

UNIT IX: Nutrition

Vitamins and Minerals

1. Vitamins are organic substances. They are derived from living matter in the form of plants, animals, or microbial sources. Minerals and their salts are non-living chemicals.
2. There is currently no scientific evidence to suggest taking extra vitamins and minerals are performance enhancing aids.
3. Groups who may need vitamin supplements:
   A. People on restricted diets.
   B. Heavy drinkers – digestive and metabolic process may be impaired or don't eat well.
   C. Pregnant and nursing women.
   D. People with intestinal disease.
   E. People taking prescription drugs that block nutrient absorption.
   F. People who cannot afford a balanced diet.
4. Most over-the-counter vitamin products today are sold as nutritional supplements, not as drugs. The regulations for foods are far less strict than those for drugs. The FDA has little control.
5. Athletes ususally consume enough calories and do not need vitamin and mineral supplements.
6. Fat soluble – can be stored in body and can produce toxic effects in large doses (A, D, E, K).
7. Water soluble – any excess is excreted in the urine.

Sports Supplements

1. Supplements that currently have scientific data to support performance enhancement include: creatine, caffeine, sodium bicarbonate, beta alanine, arginine, and dietary nitrate.
2. An estimated 4 percent of American's have used sports supplements and 1.2 million use on a regular basis.
3. It has been recommended that athletes use a carbohydrate/protein snack or supplement within 30 minutes following exercise. A high-carbohydrate meal should be consumed 2 hours after exercise to promote glycogen restoration and recovery.
4. No advanced testing need – can't claim the product will treat, prevent, or cure disease. Vague claims – enhance energy.

If You're Going to Take Vitamins

1. Don't over supplement. Choose these products with close to 100 percent of the daily values.
2. These products should be stored in a cool dark place in opaque containers.
3. Vitamins can last two to three years in a well-sealed container, and once the bottle is opened it has a 12 month shelf life.
4. The prime time to take vitamins is after meals.

Vitamin C (Ascorbic Acid)

A. Water soluble.

B. Prevents scurvy (rare in America today).

C. Helps formation of connective tissue.

D. No evidence it will prevent or cure the common cold, but may reduce the duration or severity.

E. Not effective against schizophrenia, blood clots, allergies, or bed sores.

F. Found in citrus fruits, green vegetables, tomatoes, and potatoes.

G. Dr. Linus Pauling says vitamin C decreases infections by 25% and cancers by 75% in high daily doses. Awarded Nobel prizes in chemistry and peace (banning open-air nuclear testing).

H. Has strong antioxidant properties.

Vitamin B12

A. Water soluble.

B. Production of DNA and cell replication.

C. Found in meat and dairy products.

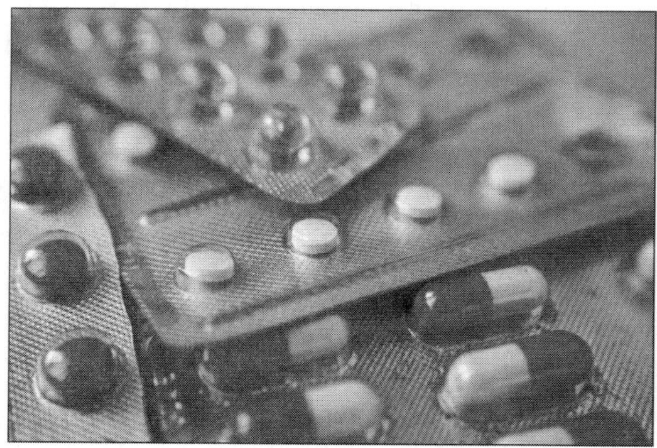

Various supplements in pill, tablet, caplet, and capsule forms.

A variety of vitamins in gel-caplet form.

Vitamin B6

A. Water soluble.

B. Requirement increases when on high protein diet, pregnant women, alcoholics, workers expose to air pollution, women on oral contraceptives.

C. Important to athletes to help the breakdown of glycogen for energy and other bodily functions.

D. Found in brewer's yeast, beef, eggs, and liver.

Vitamin B1 (Thiamine)

A. Water soluble.

B. Helps the breakdown of sugar for energy.

C. Found in yeast, rice husk, whole wheat, vegetables, and peanuts.

Vitamin B2 (Riboflavin)

A. Water soluble.

B. America's etc.

C. Found etc.

Vitamin B3 (Niacin)

A. Water soluble.

B. Involved in the production of energy, muscular, and nervous system functions.

C. Found in meats, fish, oatmeal, and bran cereal.

Vitamin B15 (Pangamic Acid)

A. Water soluble.

B. Taken off the market by the FDA as was considered carcinogenic.

C. Russians were thrilled by this drug. It was said to expand cell life, speed recovery from fatigue, ward off hangovers, and protect the liver from cirrhosis. No current U.S. scientific evidence on its effectiveness.

D. Found in brewer's yeast, whole brown rice, whole grains, pumpkin seeds, and sesame seeds.

Vitamin A

A. Fat soluble and can be toxic.

B. Essentials to maintain structure and function of all body cells.

C. Helps prevent night blindness.

D. Found in liver, carrots, vegetables, eggs, and dairy products.

Vitamin D

A. Fat soluble and can be toxic.

B. Sunshine vitamin and is produced in the skin when exposed to sunlight.

C. Helps in the formation of bones and teeth.

D. Found in fish and dairy products.

Vitamin E

A. Fat soluble.

B. Deficiency is rare.

C. Can prevent scarring from burns if applied topically.

D. Antioxidant properties.

E. Found in soybean products, nuts, cereals, etc.

Biotin

A. Water soluble.

B. Also formed naturally in the human intestine.

C. Used in digestion to breakdown and utilize fatty acids in energy metabolism.

D. Found in nuts, fruits, eggs, and milk.

Vitamin K

A. Has no ergogenic effect.

B. Used in the manufacture of blood clotting factors and building healthy bones.

C. Found in dark green vegetables, eggs, soybean, and yogurt.

Minerals

1. The human body contains more than 60 minerals and only about 22 are considered essential. Maintaining the proper percentages—not too little or not too much—may be the key to good health.

Calcium

A. Helps build bone and teeth (maintains bone density and strength). Peak bone mass is not reached until age 25 or later.

B. Insufficient calcium intake levels are a problem for most Americans.

C. Can help to prevent or minimize osteoporosis (loss of bone mass and density).

D. Found in dairy products and dark green leafy vegetables.

Chlorine

A. Helps maintain body fluids.

B. Found in table salt and fish.

Chromium

A. Used for the metabolism of carbohydrates, fats, and the regulation of glucose in blood.

B. Found in meat, whole grains, broccoli, and brewer's yeast.

Copper

A. Important in formation of red blood cells and keeps the immune system healthy.

B. Found in beans, nuts, seeds, shellfish, organ meats, and whole grains.

Fluorine

A. Is used to strengthen bones and teeth.

B. Fluoridated water.

Iodine

A. Prevents goiter and regulates thyroid gland.

B. Found in iodized salt and seafood.

Iron

A. Essential for the transportation of oxygen in the blood.

B. Prolonged exercise may deplete iron levels for endurance athletes.

C. Iron supplementation can be beneficial to iron-deficient athletes, especially if anemia is involved.

D. Found in meat, fish, eggs, liver, nuts, dried fruits, leafy green vegetables, enriched pasta, and bread.

Magnesium

A. Important in metabolic functions, bone growth, and functioning of the nerves and muscles.

B. Found in whole grains, wheat bran, dairy products, nuts, and bananas.

Manganese

A. Energy production and reproduction.

B. Found in vegetables, fruits, grains, and beans.

Phosphorus

A. Energy production, formation of bones, teeth, cell memebranes, and genetic material.

B. Found in most foods.

Potassium

A. Muscle contraction, nerve impulses, and function of the heart and kidneys.

B. Found in most foods.

Selenium

A. Act as antioxidant and may protect against cancer.

B. Found in fish, red and white meats, and eggs.

Sodium

A. Regulates water balance and blood pressure.

B. Most Americans consume too much sodium as a part of their normal diets.

C. Found in table salt and other salty foods.

Zinc

A. Needed for cell division, growth, and repair.

B. Found in seafood, meats, eggs, and dairy products.

Ginseng

1. Ginseng is a rare and expensive medicinal root which has shown some promise in combating senility in the elderly population.
2. Many products are on the market called ginseng that do not contain the root.
3. Should be taken under a physicians consent. Most of the research has been done by countries in the Far East as American research indicates little effects from the root.
4. Side effects include insomnia and hypertension, ususally seen in higher dose levels.

Ergogenic Effects

1. Chemicals called gensinosides have been said to decrease joint stiffness of aging, increase alertness and powers of concentrations, improve visual, motor coordination, and muscular oxygenation.
2. Soviet study showed young athletes increased performance capability and greater ease in performing work after nine weeks of ginseng therapy.
3. Appears to have a stimulant like effect, but improvement of athletic performance still debated int the scientific community.

Types of Protein

1. Complete protein – nine essential amino acids includes meats, poultry, seafood, eggs, milk, and cheese.
2. Incomplete protein – lacks certain essential amino acids, has to be combined with animal source protein, seeds, nuts, peas, grains, and beans.
3. Mixing complete and incomplete proteins can give you better than either one alone.
   A. 1 gram protein = 4 calories
   B. 1 gram carbohydrate = 4 calories
   C. 1 gram fat = 9 calories
4. Excess calories in the diet turn to fat.
5. Glutamine appears to have an anticatabolic effect and can be used as a supplement for athletes engaged in strenght-power sports.
6. Investigators feel athletes protein needs are:
   – 1.4 - 2.0 g/kg for strength athletes
   – 1.2 - 2.0 g/kg for endurance athletes
   – 1.2 - 1.6 g/kg for team sport athletes

Protein Supplements

1. Best formulas are derived from soybeans, which contain all essential amino acids.
2. Two tablespoons generally supply 26 grams of protein and equals a three ounce steak.
3. Increasing protein intake can benefit strength athletes or others seeking muscular gains.
4. It is suggested that athletes eat 4 to 6 meals per day and consume a carbohydrate/protein snack between meals.

Fat and Fat Manipulators

1. Lipotropics prevent abnormal or excessive accumulation of fat in the liver.
   A. Increases the liver's production of lecithin, which keeps cholesterol more soluble and helps prevent heart disease.
   B. Detoxifies the liver.
   C. Methionine, choline, inositol, and betaine are all lipotropics.

Carbohydrates and Enzymes

1. Carbohydrates are the main suppliers of our body's energy.
2. During the digestive process starches and sugars are broken down into glucose (blood sugar).
3. Carbohydrates are needed in the daily diet so protein is not wasted for energy and can be used in tissue repair.

A. Anyone on a high protein diet needs lipotropics.

4. Carbohydrate loading appears to be effective in events lasting more than one hour.

Enzymes

1. Enzymes assist in the digestion of food to release vitamins, minerals, and amino acids.
2. Each enzyme works upon a specific food.
   A. Pepsin – breaks up protein into useable amino acids.
   B. Renin – causes coagulation of milk changing its protein into a useable form in the body.
   C. Lipase – splits fat and protects the body against bruises and viral infections.
   D. Hydrochloric Acid – stomach works on tough foods; meats, vegetables, etc., causes heartburn and ulcers in excess.

Sports Drinks

1. Provide carbohydrates in a fast digesting form to supply energy to the muscles.
2. Also supplies fluids, sodium, and potassium lost in sweat during workouts and competition.

A couple of different bottled sports drinks.
(From left to right: Copyright © 2016 Everything; Copyright © 2016 yakthai)

UNIT IX

Student Activity Worksheet

Name____

Date____

Step 1

Make a list of any vitamins, mineral, or nutrional supplements you currently use or have taken in the past.

Step 2

Do or did you feel this supplement helped you in any way? Explain your answer.

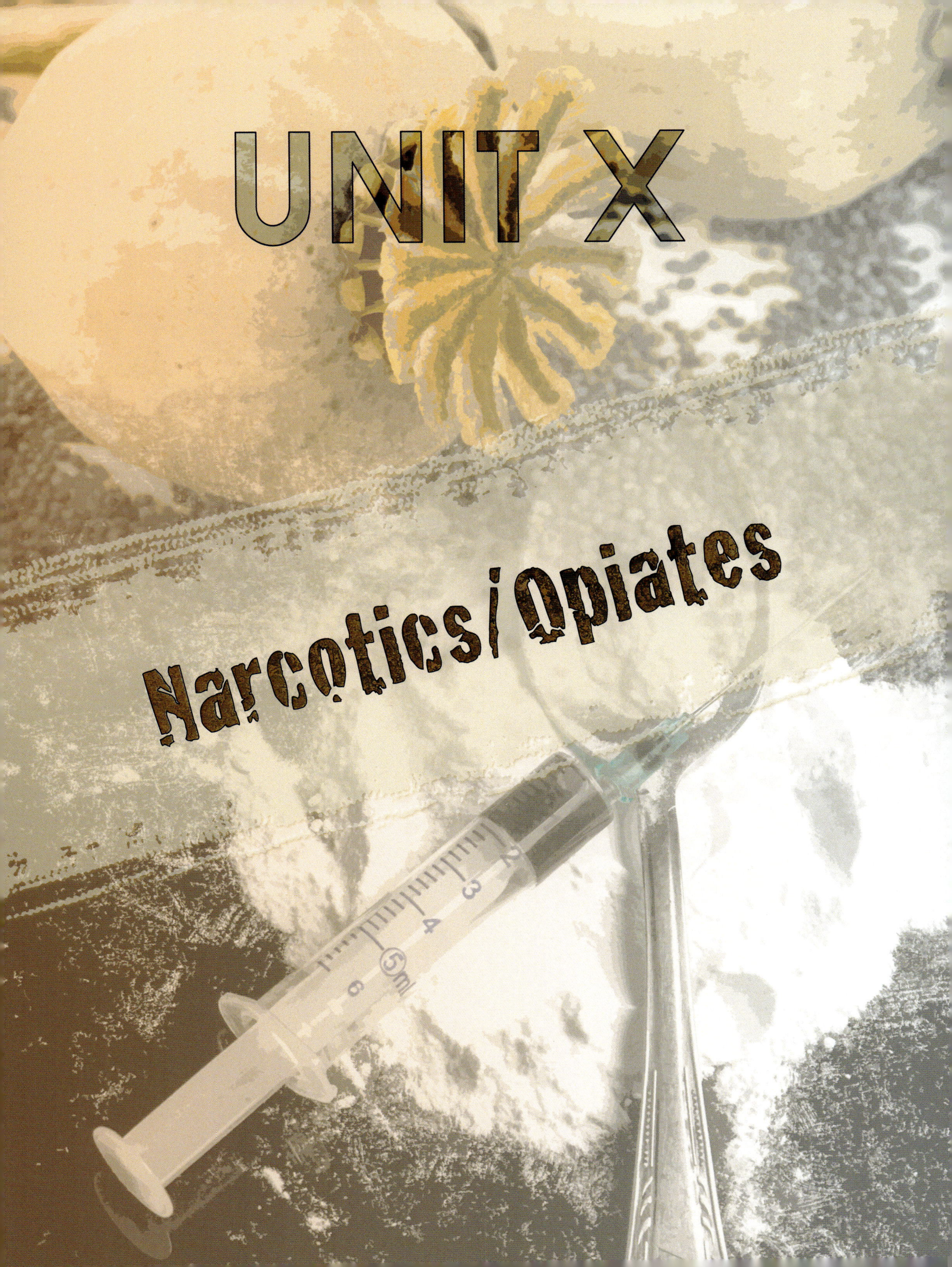
UNIT X
Narcotics/Opiates

UNIT X: Narcotics/Opiates

Narcotics

1. Medically used to kill pain and promote sleep.
   A. Best pain killers known.
   B. Also used in cough suppressants (codeine).
2. Low doses
   A. Euphoria, drowsiness, apathy
3. High doses
   A. Induces sleep, nausea, vomiting, respiratory depression, overdose
4. Usage
   A. Oral, sniffing, smoking, injection, first use is often unpleasant.
   B. Athletes may use as a pain killer from injuries; can lead to abuse and addiction.
   C. Some individuals find the need to climb to higher dosage levels and more potent drugs.
5. Hazards
   A. Contaminated drugs
   B. Contaminated needles can cause abscesses, blood poisoning, hepatitis, HIV/AIDS.
   C. Athletes recovering from injury should be aware of developing a dependence on opiates/narcotics.
6. Withdrawal
   A. Like a bad cold, symptoms disappear in seven to ten days.
   B. Can use methadone for slow withdrawal one to three weeks.
   C. Babies can be born addicted if mother is an addict when pregnant.
7. Prescription drug addiction
   A. National institute of drug abuse warns that more Americans are becoming abusers of opioid analgesics (painkillers) such as Vicodin and Oxycontin, surpassing the number of new marijuana abusers.
   B. In 2008 it was estimated that 1.85 million people in the U.S. were abusing painkillers such as Oxycontin and Vicodin.
   C. The five major painkillers (codeine, morphine, oxycodone, hydrocodone, and meperidine) retail sales rose 90% between 1997 and 2005.
   D. As the population ages, so does the need for pain medications, resulting in increased use of pain relievers.
   E. Oxycodone – common names: Oxycontin, Percodan, Darvon
   F. Hydrocodone – common name: Vicodin
   G. Meperidine – common name: Demerol

H. Treatment: inpatient/outpatient counseling, half-way house, narcotics anonymous, methadone maintenance programs. LAMM maintenance programs and narcotic antagonists use to block the effects of narcotics.

Opium

1. From the opium poppy, no restrictions in U.S. until the 1914 Harrison Narcotic Act.
2. Before medicines were labeled (Pure Food and Drug Act of 1906), people became addicted to narcotics without their knowledge as these drugs were included in various preparations.
3. Morphine and codeine are extracted from opium and used as pain killers and in cough medicine.

Morphine

1. Principal constituent of opium 4% to 21%.
2. One of the best drugs known for the relief of pain.
3. Morphine is odorless, tastes bitter, and darkens with age.
4. Tolerance and dependence develop rapidly in users.
5. Most is made into codeine.

Codeine

1. From opium ranging 0.7% to 2.5%.
2. Discovered in 1832 as an impurity in a batch of morphine.
3. Most codeine is made from morphine and is not as potent.
4. Used in cough medicine, mild pain killer.

Heroin

1. Synthesized from morphine in 1874.
2. Estimated 810,000 addicts in the U.S.
3. Methadone used in withdrawal, blocks the euphoria, and stops craving of heroin.
   A. At proper dosages a person can function without a high, but is addictive when injected or abused.
4. Usually sold "cut" or adulterated with powdered milk sugar, quinine or other materials.
5. Eventually the user doesn't even obtain a "high," they are often forced to continue using heroin to avoid the withdrawal sickness.
6. Heroin has become purer (60% to 70% purity) and cheaper than previous years. Emergency room visits and death from overdose have both increased in the U.S. in recent years.
7. Due to the cost and availability of prescription drugs, addicts may move to the use of heroin.

Signs and Symptoms of Heroin Progression*

Early Addiction Phase

The user may:
- Be introduced to other users and become curious.
- Experiment/control use "chipping," heroin often supplied by peers.
- Be exposed to blood borne infectious agents (HIV) (HBV).
- Feel urge to increase use due to feelings of euphoria and pleasurable sensations.
- Increase usage.
- Increase involvement within drug subculture, change in friends.
- Become involved with buying and selling heroin.
- Start to develop psychological need or dependence.
- Accept intervenous drug use as a way of life.

Middle Addiction Phase

The user may:
- Develop signs and symptoms of physical dependency.
- Increase tolerance; begin daily use.
- Develop family problems and dysfunctional relationships, possibly resulting in breakdown of the family unit.
- Develop job problems by increased absenteeism and loss of productivity resulting in loss of jobs.
- Become involved in criminal activity; resort to crime for extra cash needed to support increased usage.
- Experience social decay; life structure becomes chaotic, loss of self-respect, and feelings of guilt.

Late Addiction Phase

The user may:
- Increase involvement with criminal activity; increased need for drug perpetuates increased involvement with various types of crime.
- Experience deterioration of health and hygiene; total disregard for overall appearance and health habits.
- Continue usage regardless of consequences.

Choices for Continued Use

- Seek help/drug free
- Incarceration
- Death

*From: Dygert, S. and M. Minelli. "Heroin Abuse Progression Chart," *Addiction and Recovery*, 13, (1993): 27-31.

Trail of Narcotics

1. Natural origin
   A. Opium
   B. Morphine – 4% to 21 % opium

C. Codeine – 0.7% to 2.5% opium

2. Semisynthetic narcotics

A. Heroin – made from morphine

B. Thebaine derivatives (Percodan)

C. Hydromorphone (Dilaudid)

3. Synthetic narcotics

A. Meperidine (Demerol)

B. Propoxyphene (Darvon)

C. Oxycodone (Oxycontin)

D. Hydrocodone (Vicodin)

E. Methadone

F. LAAM

G. Sublimaze (Fentanyl)

H. Sublimaze – common name Fentanyl. 50 to 100 times more powerful than morphine. When mixed with other street drugs can cause overdose and death.

I. Hydromorphone – common name Dilaudid.

4. Endogenous opioids

A. Endorphins – brain's own narcotics producing euphoria and reduction of pain.

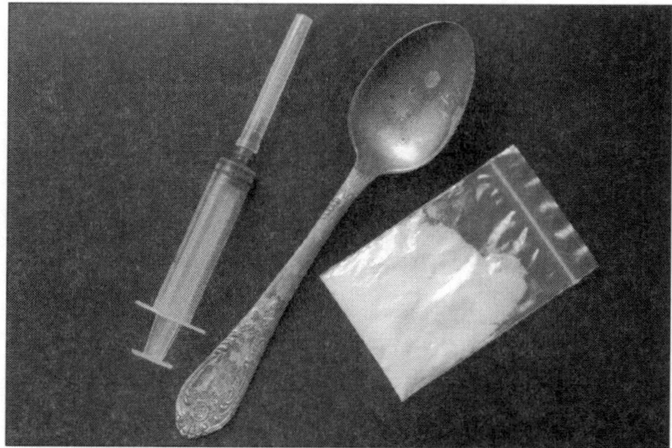

A syringe, spoon, and a bag containing heroin.
(Copyright: © 2016 Kuchina)

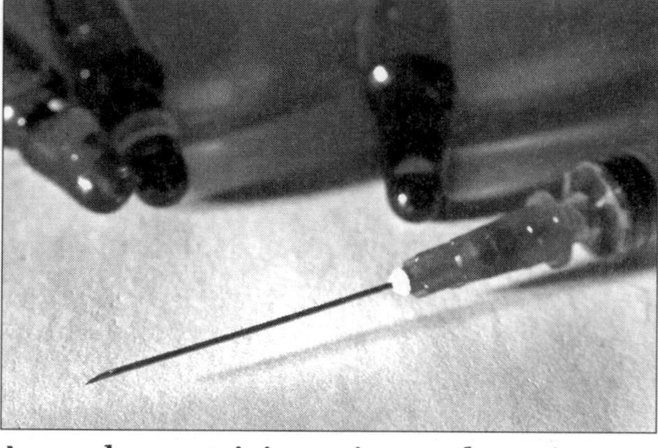

Ampoules containing opium and a syringe.
(Copyright: © 2016 Oleg Golovnev)

Vials of morphine.
(Copyright: © 2016 anaken2012)

Various forms of codeine.
(Copyright: © 2016 marylooo)

UNIT X

Student Activity Worksheet

Name____

Date____

Step 1

Consider that you are a top level research scientist and have recently invented a new medical drug. Answer the following questions:

- Name of your new drug.
- What is the drug used for?
- How is the drug taken (pill, liquid, etc.)?
- How long is the drug supposed to be taken?
- Potential side effects.
- Cost per prescription.

Step 2

Why did you invent this type of substance?

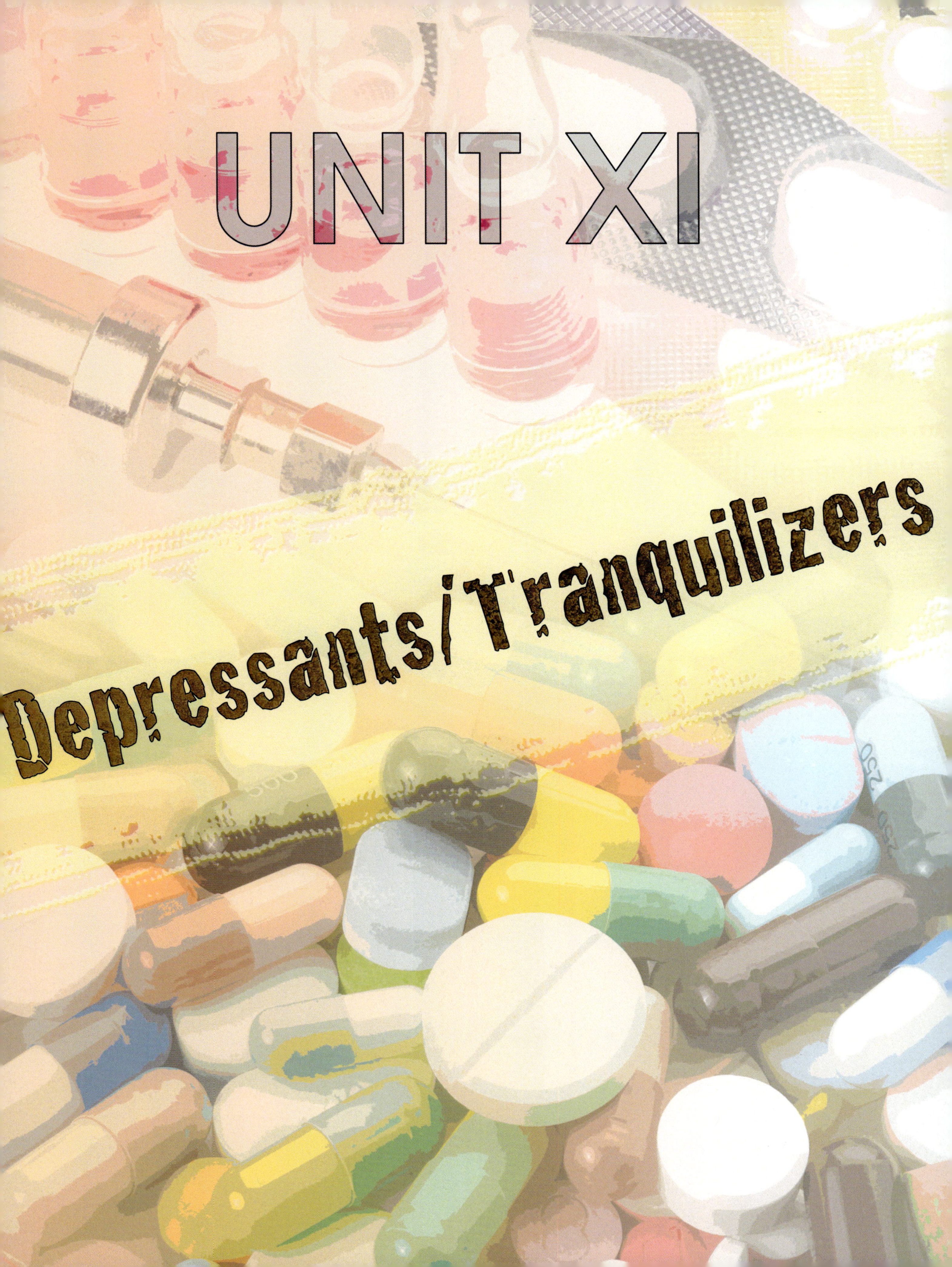
UNIT XI
Depressants/Tranquilizers

UNIT XI: Depressants/Tranquilizers

Depressants

1. Users can exhibit both physical and psychological dependence.
2. Medical uses include treatment of insomnia, relief of anxiety, irritability, and tension.
3. Too high of a dose resemble intoxicated state similar to alcohol, it may include drowsiness, sleep, stupor, coma, death, and alcohol overdose is a possibility most people are unaware of.
4. Tolerance develops rapidly.
5. Dangerous when combined with alcohol.
6. Withdrawal symptoms more severe than narcotics.
7. Barbiturates are classified as ultra-short acting, short-acting/Pentobarbital, intermediate/Seconal, long-acting/Phenobarbital.

Why Would Athletes Take Depressants?

1. Performance anxiety (to assist in sleeping the night before competition).
2. To treat a variety of medical conditions listed in this unit.
3. Depressed patients (injured athletes, losses in competition, athletes who's careers are over sometimes become depressed).
4. Countering the effects of a stimulant.
5. Note: athletes and professional entertainers sometimes face the same life issues and may use some of the substances in this manual for similar reasons.

Minor Tranquilizer's (Sedative-Hypnotics)

1. Developed in the 1950's as antianxiety agents.
2. Most came out in the 1960's as a family of drugs called Benzodiazepenes. Most famous are Librium, Serax, Valium, Tranxene, and Dalmone.
3. Companies said they were revolutionary drugs to reduce anxiety, but are similar to alcohol with adverse effects and dependence.
4. Medical uses include:
   - A. Relief of tension and anxiety.
   - B. Acute alcohol withdrawal – DT's (Delirium Tremens)
   - C. Relief of skeletal muscle spasm.
   - D. Spasticity from Cerebral Palsy, etc.
   - E. Convulsive disorders – Epilepsy
   - F. Treat hallucinogen induced panic reactions.
   - G. Induce sleep.

H. Virtually suicide proof unless mixed with other central nervous system (CNS) depressants.

5. Side effects include:
   A. Physical and psychological dependence.
   B. Withdrawal upon abrupt discontinuance.
   C. Dangerous when operating machinery, driving motor vehicles.
   D. Mixed with alcohol or other CNS depressants can be dangerous.
   E. Increased risk of congenital malformations to the fetus.
6. Sometimes called "don't give a damn pills," people just don't care.

Major Tranquilizers

1. Known as the antischizophrenics, antipsychotics.
2. Includes Phenothiazines – Thorazine, Mellaril, Stelazine, and Haldol.
3. Most major tranquilizers seems to be effective, there is no best drug. They are nonaddictive.
4. Medically used for:
   A. Control of nausea and vomiting.
   B. Control of manic-depressive illness.
   C. Control restlessness and apprehension before surgery.
   D. Adjunct treatment to tetanus.
   E. Mild alcohol withdrawal.
   F. Hyperactivity or aggressiveness in disrupted children.
5. Side effects include:
   A. Not determinded safe during pregnancy.
   B. May impair mental or physical abilities.
   C. Not safe if used with alcohol or other sedatives.
   D. Muscle tremors, weakness, drooling.
   E. Hypertension.
   F. Allergic reactions of the skin, jaundice.
   G. Dry mouth.
   H. Breast enlargement.

Muscle Relaxants

1. Common drugs include Flexeril, Norgesic, Parafon Forte, Robaxin.
2. Medically used for:
   A. Muscle spasms or stiffness.

B. Muscle pulls, sprains, cramps.
C. Control pain of arthritis, dental procedures, menstruation.

3. Side effects include:
   A. Impairs mental and physical abilities.
   B. Drowsiness.
   C. Dry mouth.
   D. Weakness.
   E. Not safe during pregnancy.
   F. Rapid heartbeat.
   G. Rashes.
   H. Blurred vision.
   I. Nausea.
   J. Lightheadedness.

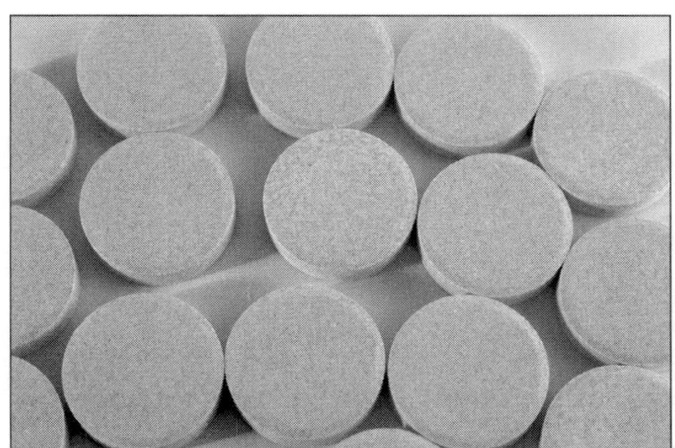

Minor tranquilizer: valium.

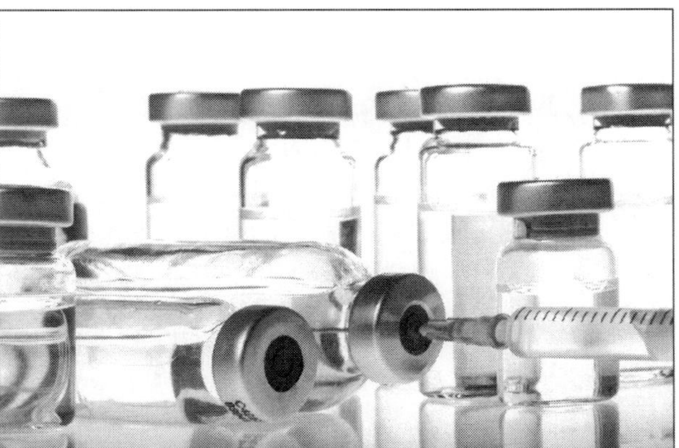

Major tranquilizer: haldol.

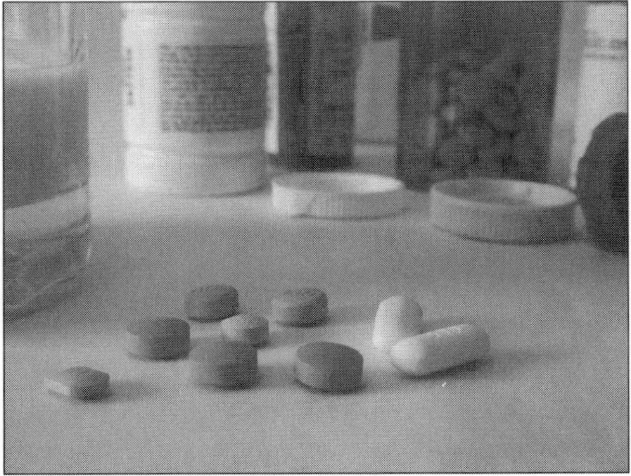

Various muscle relaxants.

UNIT XI

Student Activity Worksheet

Name________________________________

Date________________________________

Step 1

Make a list of what you do to reduce stress in your life.

Step 2

What other activities or things would you try that would help reduce stress in your life?

UNIT XII

Drugs, Hormones, and Other Non-Nutritional Aids

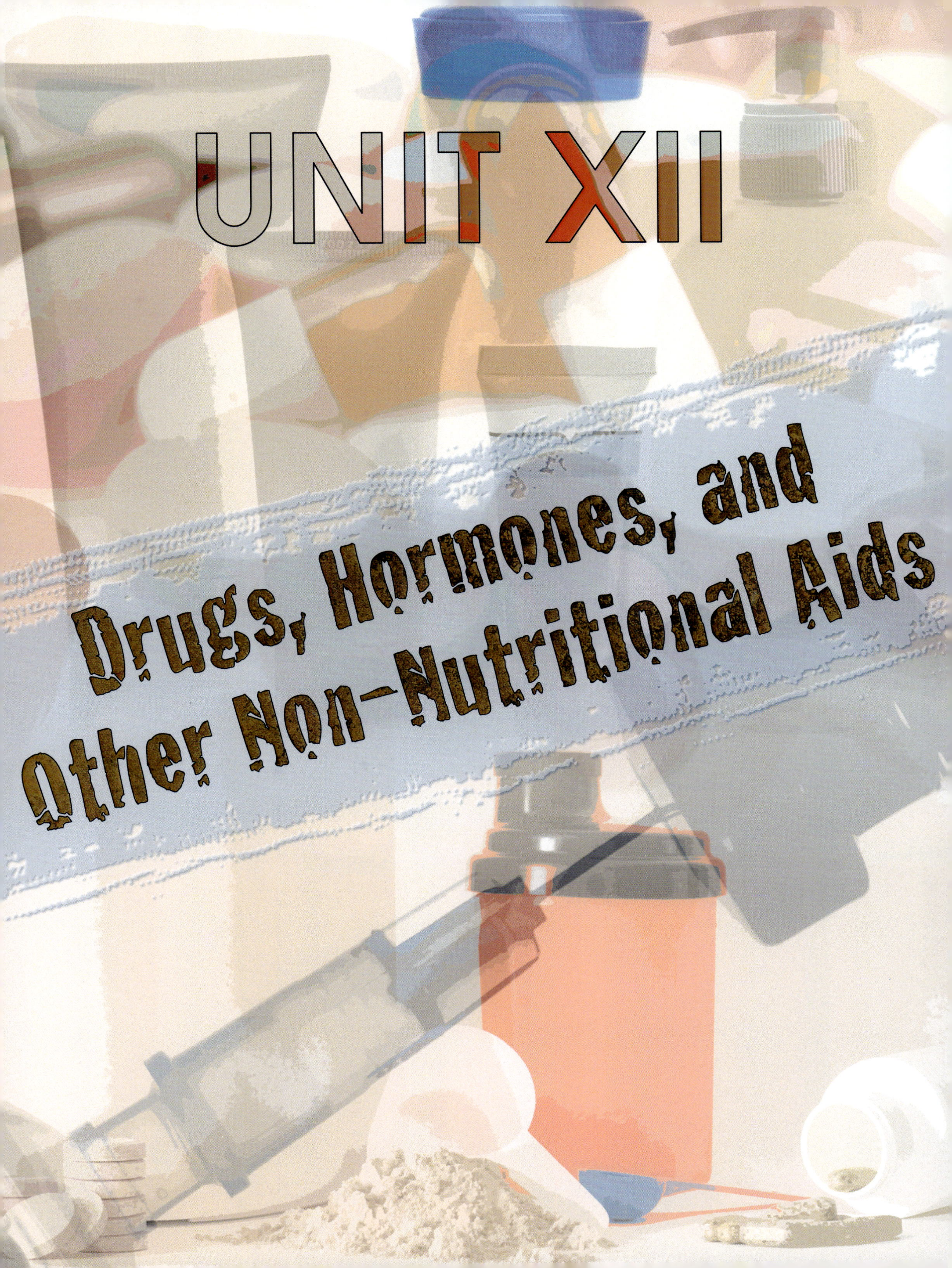

UNIT XII: Drugs, Hormones, and Other Non-Nutrional Aids

Estrogen (Birth Control Pills)

1. Estrogen is the female sex hormone available by prescription only in tablets, injection, or vaginal creams.
2. Medically used for:
   A. Prevention of pregnancy.
   B. Regulation of the menstrual cycle.
   C. Relief of symptoms due to menopause.
3. Side effects include:
   A. Retention of fluid, gain in weight.
   B. Bleeding or spotting in middle of menstrual cycle.
   C. Change in menstrual flow.
   D. Increase susceptibility to yeast infection of the genital tissues.
   E. Extended use can cause tumors of the uterus or cancer in the lining of the uterus.
4. Caution should be taken if the user has:
   A. Allergic reaction to these drugs.
   B. Impaired liver function.
   C. History of heart problems, stroke, embolism, etc.
   D. History of cancer of breast or reproductive organs
   E. Diabetes.
   F. A habit of smoking.
   G. Female athletes should note studies showing a decrease in ability to repair muscles following intense eccentric exercise. This can lead to poorer performance, so athletes should monitor this if using estrogen.

Diuretics

1. Prescription is required, sometimes called water pills.
2. Medically used for:
   A. Elimination of excessive fluid retention (edema).
   B. Reduction of high blood pressure.
3. Increases the elimination of salt and water through increased urine production. Reduces body fluids and lowers sodium content. Increased urine volume begins in two hours, reaches maximum in four to six hours.
4. Caution should be taken if the user is:
   A. Allergic to sulfa drugs.

B. Pregnant.

C. Has a history of kidney or liver disease.

D. Diabetic.

5. Side effects include:

A. Weakness.

B. Drowsiness.

C. Muscle pains and cramps.

D. Muscle fatigue.

E. Frequent urination (can lead to dehydration).

F. Rash or hives.

G. Nausea, vomiting, and loss of appetite.

H. Heat injury.

6. Extended use can cause:

A. Impaired balance of water (dehydration), salt, and potassium in the blood and body tissues.

B. Development of diabetes in predisposed individuals.

7. Other issues:

A. Need to eat foods rich in potassium if on diurectics; bananas, meats, carrots, etc.

B. Heavy exercise or exertion while on this drug can cause muscle cramps, fatigue, and raise blood pressure.

C. Common brand names include Diuril, Duretic, Saluron, and Thiuretic.

8. Ergogenic effects:

A. Mask other drugs in urine.

B. Lose weight quickly which is helpful in many sports.

Laxatives

1. Laxatives are used when costipation is frequent or patients experience difficult evacuation of feces. Laxatives have been found to relieve this condition.

2. Normal bowel functions:

A. Many people believe you need one bowel movement a day. This is only a myth.

B. Research indicates normal is three per day down to three a week, so unless you are not in this range there is no need to increase or decrease the number.

C. Laxatives are sometimes used by wrestlers to "make weight."

3. Constipation:

A. Usually caused by poor diet, inadequate intake of dietary fiber, or too little water and other fluids.

B. Laxatives should be a temporary measure only. They should not be used on a regular basis or extended period of time.

   C. Any sudden change in bowel habits that persists for two weeks should be reported to a physician.

4. Types of laxatives:
   A. Bulk-forming laxatives increase the stool's bulk volume and water content. Experts feel they are one of the safest types of laxatives.
   B. Stimulant laxatives stimulate peristalsis in the large and small intestine to move fecal matter along. They should not be used daily for more than a week. Overdosage or persistent use can produce serious side effects. Dependence on laxatives can make it difficult to have a bowel movement without the drug.
   C. Saline refers to salt and is believed to pull water into the intestine. Serious loss of body salts can result from use, so take this only occasionally.
   D. Hyperosmotic laxatives attracts water into the stool, similar to saline type with the same side effects.
   E. Stool softener penetrates and softens the stool. Use no longer than one week.
   F. Lubicant laxatives do what they say: lubricate. Mineral oil is a natural lubricant.

Ergogenic Effects

1. Sometimes used to lose weight quickly for a variety of sports.

Blood Doping

1. This process is done by withdrawing 800 to 1200 ml of whole blood and then storing it in a blood bank. After four of five weeks when the hemoglobin concentration (and performance) has returned to normal, the red blood cells are reinfused.
2. Side effects include:
   A. Syncope or loss of consciousness due to inadequate blood flow to the brain.
   B. Hematoma formation (which is a blood clot confined to an organ, tissue, or space caused by a break in a blood vessel).
   C. Infection due to a variety of problems associated with the storage, reinfusion process, or of possibly infected blood.
   D. Blood volume overload (increased cardiac work).
3. Ergogenic effects:
   A. Maximal aerobic power can increase by ten percent (less in highly trained athletes). Effects last from one to eighteen days.
   B. Maximal aerobic power and improved physical performance is shown in large muscle groups used during prolonged exercise only.

Erythropoietin

1. This drug stimulates the bone marrow to produce additional red blood cells and is used to treat anemia. It is also a naturally occurring hormone.
2. Side effects include:
   A. Thickened blood begins to clot and can result in heart attack and stroke.

3. Ergogenic effects:
   A. Theoretically erythropoietin could enhance oxygen transport for endurance events (i.e., runners, cyclists, and cross-country skiers).
   B. Easier and more effective way to blood dope.

Dimethyl Sulfoxide (DMSO)

1. Although athletes sometime use this substance to reduce swelling, there are no proven ergogenic effects on human test subjects. DMSO usually comes in a gel for topical application and is used by veterinarians to decrease local swelling secondary to trauma.
2. Side effects include:
   A. Garlic odor and taste in mouth.
   B. Localized skin irritation.
   C. Contaminants may be absorbed when applied on skin.
   D. Athletes using veterinary dosage levels of DMSO increase the potential for serious health hazards. Many athletes obtain black market animal versions of DMSO.
   E. This drug needs to be studied further before we can make any assumptions about its safety for use in humans.

Beta Blockers

1. These drugs dilate blood vessels, relax the nonvascular smooth muscle of the bronchioles and intestine, stimulate the heart, and help break down fat and starch for energy.
2. Can be medically used to treat arrhythmia, hypertension, anxiety states, migraine headaches, and drug withdrawal.
3. Side effects include:
   A. Fluid in the heart.
   B. Slowed heart rate.
   C. Low blood pressure.
   D. Male impotence.
   E. Hair loss.
   F. Gastrointestinal disturbances.
   G. Various withdrawal symptoms.
4. Ergogenic effects:
   A. Used by athletes to decrease anxiety and heart rate and increase concentration and control for sports such as pistol, rifle shooting, archery, or golf.

Beta-2 Agonists

1. Used therapeutically for treatment of asthma and symptoms of the common cold.

2. Could be used by athletes for the bronchodilation effects increasing aerobic capacity.
3. Some beta-2 agonists can exhibit anabolic effects (clenbuterol).
4. Evidence showing anti-inflammatory effects.
5. Some beta-2 agonists are banned in sports if not taken as directed from the manufacturer for inhalation (asthma treatments).
6. Side effects include:
   A. Tachycardia.
   B. Cardiac arrhythmias.
   C. Increased susceptibility to infections due to bronchodilation.

Carnitine

1. Found in most cells of the human body and facilitates the trasportaion of fatty acids into mitochondrea (powerhouse cells) for oxidation.
2. The oxidation process releases energy in the form of adenosine triphosphate (ATP) for muscle concentration.
3. Studies to date indicate that carnitine has mixed results as an ergogenic aid. Medical risks with doses currently used appear to be minimal.
4. Two types of carnitine are found in supplements: L-carnitine and D-carnitine. While L-carnitine appears to be safe, D-carnitine can actually create a deficiency of this substance in the human body and thus cause muscle weakness. As carnitine is produced in the human body, supplementaion could cause problems or do nothing to promote enhanced performance.
5. Ergogenic effects:
   A. Carnitine may enhance intensive exercise performance.

Sodium Bicarbonate (Baking Soda)

1. Sometimes referred to as bicarbonate doping, buffer boosting, soda doping, and soda loading. This product is also available from pharmacies via capsules.
2. Used to (in theory) rid the muscle of lactic acid delaying muscle fatigue (currently debated in scientific studes).
3. Side effects include:
   A. Excessive loss of acids from body fluids.
   B. Apathy, confusion, stupor, or muscle spasms.
   C. Gastrointestinal discomfort or rapid onset diarrhea (less if used via capsules).
   D. Ingestion appears to be most effective during maximal exercise bouts between one and seven minutes.
4. Ergogenic effects:
   A. Used by athletes in the 400 to 800 meter runs and 100 to 200 meter swims.

B. Some studies indicate no ergogenic effects while others show improved racing times.

C. A dosage of 300 mg/kg bodyweight has consistently shown to increase maximal exercise duration.

D. Ingestion appears to be most effective during maximal exercies bouts—between one to seven minutes.

Phosphate Salts

1. Phosphate salts have been used by athletes for over 50 years to increase energy production.
2. The effectiveness is debated as some studies have shown reduced lactic acid levels during exercise and improved oxygen to muscles. Other studies have not.
3. Does not appear to pase any significant medical risk.

Oxygen

1. Used to (in theory) increase hemoglobin or oxygen levels in blood (not proven by scientific evidence).
2. Arterial hemoglobin is almost 100 percent in normal situations, so it can only be a placebo effect.

Creatine

1. Creatine is a naturally occurring compound produced by the liver and stored in the brain, skeletal and cardiac muscle, sperm, and certain cells of the immune system.
2. Manufactured in the body from two nonessential amino acids: arginine and glycine.
3. Highest concentrations in food found in raw meat and fish. Cooking reduces creatine levels. It is not practical to do creatine loading through normal diet as it would take approximately five pounds of raw meat to creatre the proper effect.
4. At present, no significant side effects have been reported in the clinical trials that have been conducted. Some athletes have noted increased blood pressure, probably from over supplementation, muscle cramping, nausea, gastrointestinal disturbances, elevated liver enzymes, and kidney damage.
5. A common method of supplementation used is a 5- or 6-day loading period, consisting of approximately 20 grams of creatine per day. Impurities have been found in virtually every maufactured product.
6. Ergogenic effects:

   A. May improve running in 3 ways:

      1. Stored in energy pools in skeletal muscle, creatine functions like a high-voltage battery to provide almost instantaneous energy for explosive muscle movements (short duration events).

2. High creatine levels can delay fatigue during short intense efforts, such as uphill running, mid-race surges, track workouts, and finishing kicks.
3. Creatine phosphate serves as a shuttle of energy from the mitochondria (cells where most energy reactions occur) to your muscles.

B. Creatine's potential benefits are most advantageous in short races; beyond 5K effects are much less significant. Weightlifters and bodybuilders are now using creatine to build body mass (probably due to water retention).

C. Creatine is not a currently banned substance, but no guarantees can be made because this foreign-made product may very in its composition.

D. Studies have not yet determined if prolonged creatine supplementation is safe. Caution should be taken in its use.

E. Short-term studies (5 years or less) indicate that creatine supplementation does not appear to pose a health risk when taken as recommended.

Dehydroepiandrosterone (DHEA)

1. Produced by both sexes in the adrenal glands and helps fuel the production of sex hormones, particularly testosterone. DHEA is a precursor to testosterone (which convers to steroids only after they are ingested).
2. Currently sold as an over-the-counter supplement.
3. Problems may occur as strength and purity are not regulated and long-term clinical trials have not been done. No scientific proof of muscle gains.
4. Side effects include:
   A. Acne.
   B. Hair loss.
   C. Excessive hair growth and deepening of the voice in females.
   D. Potential cancer of the prostate and breast.
5. Potential ergogenic effects:
   A. Improves mood.
   B. Increased energy and libido.
   C. Reduced stress hormone levels.
   D. Anti-aging effects preserving muscle quality.
   E. May strengthen immune system response.

Chromium Picolinate

1. Currently being advertized as a safe anabolic nutrient. Claims state no side effects or toxicities notes in clinical studies.
2. Studies have indicated that chromium has no beneficial ergogenic effects.
3. Found naturally in mushrooms, prunes, nuts, whole-grain and cereal, and brewer's yeast.

Unique Ergogenic Aids

Thermojetics – Ma-Huang (stimulant) banned by the U.S. Olympic Committee. Deaths due to overdose have been reported.

Mexican Yam – no ergogenic effect reported and is not currently a banned substance.

Gamma-Oryzanol – no ergogenic effect reported and is not currently a banned substance.

Syndocarb (Mesocarb) – the Soviet Union believed it to be effective in increasing muscle workload with little or no effect on the cardiovascular system. This substance may show up as a stimulant during drug testing.

Q 10 – currently considered a vitamin and is legally sold without medical claims as a dietary supplement. Not banned by regulatory groups.

Herbal Plant Sterols – naturally ingested plant sterols cannot be converted into testosterone in the human body. It is not currently banned.

Formul-One – contains a variety of stimulants such as ephedrine, caffeine, and other compounds that may jeopardize safety and ability to pass a drug test.

Melatonin – no ergogenic effect reported and is not currently a banned substance.

Jin Bu Huan – a chinese herb with morphine like properties. May show up as a narcotic on a drug screening test.

Cordyceps Sinensis

1. A Chinese mushroom said to build physical stamina, mental energy, and sexual power. Active ingredients are cordycepin, other oligosaccharides, and amino acids.
2. Chinese women's long-distance team broke world records in 1992 and their coach gave much credit to this substance. All of the athletes passed thier drug tests.
3. Current research is not conclusive with mixed results as an ergogenic aid.
4. Athletes need to be aware that many fake products are available.
5. This supplement is not banned at present.

Plant Extracts

1. Green coffee extract and Garcinia Cambogia has been marketed as an appetite suppressant.
2. Data on these supplements is inconclusive with some research showing weight loss and appetite suppression other studies no results.

Androstendione

1. Androstendione is produced in the body from either 17-ahydroxyprogesterone or DHEA. One study found that andro increased testosterone levels twice as much as DHEA. This substance could be used to restore lowered testosterone levels in aging men and women.

2. East Germany used it to enhance performance of elite athletes. It was later refined for use in a nasal spray to increase plasma testosterone levels and still remain undetected in Olympic drug testing.
3. A recent U.S. study indicated andro does nothing to boost men's strength or serum testosterone levels and, instead, may promote breast enlargement, heart disease, and cancer.

Manufacturer's Claims

1. Poor – testimonials, advertising brochures, and manufacturer's information.
2. Questionable – small group studies, individual reports, studies using non-athletes or beginners, and few specific details in the study cited.
3. Valid – used trained athletes in the study, involved adequate number of subjects (15 to 20 minimum), study details provided, doses appear reasonable, random and experimental control groups used, and statistical analysis of data.

A variety of hormone-infused creams.
(Copyright: © 2016 mihalec)

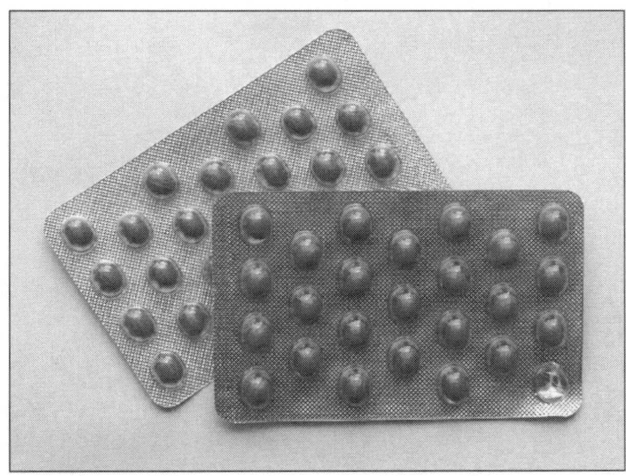

Packages of a diuretic in pill form.
(Copyright: © 2016 Claudio Divizia)

Various non-nutritional aids.
(Copyright: © 2016 CobraCZ)

UNIT XII

Student Activity Worksheet

Name____

Date____

Step 1

Should student-athletes be allowed to use performance enhancing drugs or methods? Should these substances continue to be regulated? Explain your answers.

UNIT XIII
Behavioral Health Concerns of Athletes

UNIT XIII: Behavioral Health Concerns of Athletes

Gambling Among Student-Athletes

1. Research indicates the lifetime pathological gambling rates in college students is approximately 5.6%.
2. Research suggest that student-athletes may be vulnerable to gambling problems. The NCAA has done surveys on student-athletes in 2004, 2008, and 2012. 22 sports were reviewed in three divisions. Detailed analysis can be viewed in the online report "NCAA Student-Athlete Gambing Behaviors and Attitudes: 2004-2012," Supplementary Tables, May 2013.
3. Gambling appears to activate the pleasure centers of the brain. Repeated gambling may result in long-term brain changes similar to that seen in other addictive behaviors.
4. If gambling causes problems for the student-athlete financially, legally, with family or friends, or with progress in academics, one should seek help (i.e., counseling, Gambler's Anonymous, state councils on problem and compulsive gambling, coaches).

Eating Disorders

1. In general athletes have been found to be more at risk of developing an eating disorder than the general population. Prevalence is higher in females and increases if the sport has a weight requirement or appearance is emphasized.
2. The reduction in food intake when athletes have an eating disorder can result in risk to health, lowered performance level, and overall risk of injury.
3. Causes of eating disorders are complex, but are believed to relate to genetics, social pressures, and psychological issues.
4. Warning signs of eating disorders in athletes can include:
   A. Concern or preoccupation with food intake and weight gain.
   B. Reading and intense study of food lables reviewing calories and fat content.
   C. Making excuses for not eating with others and eating alone.
   D. Excessive exercies programs, even beyond athletic requirements.
   E. Wearing baggy clothing to hide weight loss.
   F. Cutting food into very small bites, excessive chewing, and playing with food on plate.
   G. Trips to the bathroom during or after meals (person may vomit food).
   H. Food binges followed by purging behaviors.
5. Two major eating disorders are:
   A. Anorexia Nervosa – which includes extensive weight loss through self-starvation, which can be life-threatening.

B. Bulimia Nervosa – noted as binging and purging food and can also be life-threatening.

6. Treatment recommended is often the three sphere approach: psychological/medical/nutritional.

Athletes Facing Depression–When the Performance Career is Finished

1. At some point, all athletes will complete their playing career. This can be a very difficult time. Former athletes may require a psychological adjustment in their lives. Some people believe their identity is being an athlete.
2. Clues to look for when athletes are depressed or grieve the loss of their sport:
   A. Sleeping too much or too little. Waking throughout the night.
   B. Changes in eating behaviors leading to weight loss or gain.
   C. Daily activities seem boring. A loss of pleasure.
   D. Angry at loss of playing their sport. Has little interest in becoming a spectator.
   E. Complaints of being tired and loss of energy.
   G. Abusive drinking patterns or drug use.
3. Treatment
   A. Treatment of depression is highly effective and usually involves counseling and medications.

Gene Doping–Will Athletes Be Tempted to Enhance Performance?

1. In sports, it could be used to:
   A. Enhance normal human traits.
   B. Improve muscle performance.
   C. Function as erythropoietin (blood cell production) oxygen delivery to exercising tissues.
   D. Increase energy production.
   E. Treat disease and repair injuries.
2. Three methods currently researched: gene therapy; gene transfer; gene enhancement.
3. Gene Transfer – potential to treat cancer, HIV/AIDS, neurodegenerative diseases, cardiovascular disease, diabetes, and genetic diseases.
4. Normal genes could be injected into the body to increase tissue function.
5. This process is still in the experimental phase. Success is very low and risks are still high.
6. As with other ergogenic methods, the placebo effect of gene doping could enhance performance.
7. Detection to find cheaters is possible and will improve as new methods of gene doping appear on the sports scene.

8. Would parents or countries be tempted to create super humans?
9. Although there is no evidence to date that athletes have successfully used gene doping procedures, regulating bodies believe it will come in the future.
10. Inhibiting myostatin for muscle growth.
    A. To inhibit myostatin through the use of gene doping could be an important development for the production of increased muscle growth in the future.
    B. Although modifying myostatin agents are banned, to this date there are no products available to create this effect.
    C. Experimentation with animals has shown increased muscle mass development.

The allure of gambling can be addictive.
(Copyright: © 2016 alfexe)

Gene doping may be the wave of the future.
(Copyright: © 2016 Fisher Photostudio)

Animal with inhibiting myostatin growth.
(Public domain image)

UNIT XIII

Student Activity Worksheet

Name____

Date____

Step 1

Do you believe student-athletes are under additional psychological pressures in comparison to other college students? Explain your answer.

School-Based Guidelines and Policy on Substance Abuse by Student-Athletes

Written Policy

Describes the school policy. Provided to all student-athletes and parents at beginning of school year.

Education Program

Offer an education session or series of classes to all student-athletes prior to each season of competition. Keep student-athletes actively involved in all class sessions. Alternatives to using these drugs along with short and long term health consequences of use should be incorporated into the class discussions.

Identification

Provide educational sessions on how to identify student-athletes with substance abuse problems to all coaches, trainers, and other professional staff.

Early Intervention/Rehabilitation

Develop due-process procedures and require counseling or other rehabilitative services for student-athletes using steroids and other drugs.

Note: adapted from Guidelines of Establishing a Policy on Substance Abuse by Student/Athletes by National Association For Sport and Physical Education, 1989.

This information is reprinted with permission form the Journal of Physical Education, Recreation & Dance, October, 1992, 68-74. JOPERD is a publication of The American Alliance For Health, Physical Education, Recreation & Dance, 1900 Association Drive, Reston, VA, 22091.

NCAA List of Banned Substances 2014-2015

List of NCAA banned drug classes and procedures 2014-2015 (by major categories only). See NCAA for most current listing at www.ncaa.org/health-safety/policy/2014-15-ncaa-banned-drugs.

Caffeine – if the concentration in urine exceeds 15 micrograms/ml

Amphetamine, ephedrine (ephedra, ma huang)

Cocaine

Anabolic-androgenic steroids (includes, but not limited to):
Testosterone
Stanozolol
Clenbuterol
Androstenedione
DHEA

Substances banned for specific sports (includes, but not limited to):
Alcohol
Diuretics and other masking agents
Street drugs
Heroin
Marijuana (THC)
Blood doping
Growth Hormone (HGH)
Beta-blockers (for riflery only)
Erythropoietin (EPO)
Manipulation of urine samples
Human chorionic gonadotrophin (HCG)
Ant-estrogens
Beta-2 agonists – permitted by prescription and inhalation

The World Anti-Doping Code
The 2015 Prohibited List
International Standard

Substances and methods prohibited at all times (in and out of competition).

Short Listing of Prohibited Substances and Procedures—see full listing at the World Anti-Drug Agency.

Anabolic androgenic steroids/agents

Peptide hormones, growth factors, related substances and mimetics

Beta-2 agonists

Hormone and metabolic modulators

Diuretics and masking agents

Manipulation of blood and blood components

Chemical and physical manipulation

Gene doping

Stimulants

Narcotics

Cannabinoids

Glucocorticoids

Alcohol

Beta-blockers

Selected Web Sites

The author does not endorse these Web sites, but provides them as information only.

Facts on Tap – **www.factsontap.org**

National Center For Responsible Gaming – **www.ncrg.org**

The Bacchus Network – **www.bacchusnetwork.org**

National Institutes of Health /National Institute on Alcohol Abuse and Alcoholism – **www.niaaa.nih.gov**

Prevention Network – **www.preventionnetwork.org**

Healthfinder – **www.healthfinder.gov**

National Institutes of Health – **www.nih.gov**

Academy of Nutrition and Dietetics – **www.eatright.org**

Fitnesslink – **www.fitnesslink.com**

National Eating Disorders Association – **www.nationaleatingdisorders.org**

U.S. National Agricultural Library – **www.nalusda.gov**

Substance Abuse & Mental Health Services Administration – **www.samhsa.gov**

Center For Substance Abuse Prevention – **www.covesoft.com/csap.html**

Alcoholics Anonymous – **www.alcoholics-anonymous.org**

Narcotics Anonymous – **www.wsoinc.com**

National Institute on Drug Abuse – **www.steroidabuse.org**

NCAA – **www.ncaa.org/references**

The Taylor Hooton Foundation Fighting Steroid Abuse – **www.taylorhooton.org/home**

World Anti-Doping Agency – **www.wada.ama.org/en/index.ch2**

U.S. Anti-Doping Agency – **www.usantidoping.org/default.aspx**

References

Abramowicz, M. (ed). "Dehydroepiandrosterone (DHEA)," *The Medical Letter*, 38, (1996): 91-92.

Akl, E., Gunukula, S., and S. Aleem. "The Prevalence of Waterpipe Tobacco Smoking Among the General and Specific Populations: A Systematic Review," *BMC Public Health*, 2010, 11, (2010):244-255.

American College Health Association, *Action*, 34, 1, July/August/September, 1994.

American College of Sports Medicine Position Stand. Blood Doping as an Ergogenic Aid, *Med Sci Sports Exerc*, 5, (1987): 540-543.

Anderson, W.A., Albrecht, R.R. and D.B. McKeag. Second Replication of a National Study of the Substance Abuse Habits of College Student Athletes, unpublished report, July 30, 1993.

Anshel, M., *Sports Psychology From Theory to Practice*, Scottsdale, AZ, Gorsuch Scarisbrick Publisher, 1994.

Anshel, M. "Toward Development of a Model For Coping With Acute Stress in Sport," *International J Sport*, 21 (1990): 58-83.

Antonio, J. and J. Stout. *Sports Supplements*. Philadelphia, Lippincott, Williams and Wilkins, 2001.

Astell, K., Mathai, M., Su., X. et al. "Plant Extracts With Appetite Suppressing Properties For Body Weight Control: A Systematic Review of Double Blind Randomized Controlled Clinical Trials," *Comp Therapies in Medicine*, 21, (2013): 407-416.

"Attention: Aging Men," *Newsweek*, 16 September 1996.

Avis, H. *Drugs & Life*. Dubuque, Iowa, WM. C. Brown Publishers, 1990.

Balsom, P.D. "Creatine Supplementation Per Se Does Not Enhance Endurance Exercise Performance," *ACTA Physical Scand.*, 149, (1993): 521-3.

Benardot, D. *Advanced Sports Nutrition*. Champaign, IL: Human Kinetics, 2006.

Benedikt, R., Cristofaro, P., Mendelson, J., and N. Mello. "Effects of Acute Marijuana Smoking in Postmenopausal Women," *Psychopharmacology*, 90, (1986): 14-17.

Bernstein, J. Medical Consequences of Marihuana Use. In Mello, N. (ed). *Advances in Substance Abuse, Behavioral and Biological Research*. Greenwich, CT, Jai Press, 1980.

Berry, C. and D. Wagner. "Effect of Pseudoephedrine on 800-m-run Times of Female Collegiate Track Athletes," *Med & Science in Sports & Exer*, 43 (5), (2011), Suppl 1:853.

Bhasin, S., Storer, T.W., Berman, N., et al. "The Effects of Supraphysiologic Doses of Testosterone On Muscle Size and Strength In Normal Men," *N Engl J Med*, 335 (1996): 1-8.

Bianco, A., Thomas, E., Pomara, F., et al. "Alcohol Consumption and Hormonal Alterations Related to Muscle Hypertrophy: A Review," *Nutrition and Metabolism*, 11, (2014): 26, dio:10.1186/1743-7075-11-43.

"Biology, Addiction, and Gambling." *The Wager*, 8,35, August 27, 2003. Retrieved: 9/2/03, from: http://www.thewager.org/current.htm.

Blum, K., Noble, E., Sheridan, P., et al. "Allelic Association of Human Dopamine D2 Receptor Gene In Alcoholism," *JAMA*, 263, (1990): 2055-2060.

Borum, P. "Carnitine In Human Nutrition," *Nutrition and the M.D.*, 9, (1982): 1.

Braude, A. "Transfusion Reactions From Contaminated Blood: Their Recognition and Treatment," *N Engl J Med*, 258, (1958): 1289-1293.

Brechier, E. *Licit and Illicit Drugs*. Boston, Little, Brown and Co., 1972.

Bucci, L. *Nutrients as Ergogenic Aids For Sports and Exercise*, Boca Raton, FL, CRC Press Inc., 1993.

Buckley, W., Yesalis, C. III., Friedl, K., et al. "Estimated Prevalence of Anabolic Steroid Use Among Male High School Seniors," *JAMA*, 23, (1988): 3441-3445.

Burfoot, A. and G. Hirsch. "Coming of Age," *Runners World*, 22, (1987): 56-61.

Campbell, W., Joseph, L., Davey, S., et al. "Effects of Resistance Training and Chromium Picolinate On Body Composition and Skeletal Muscle In Older Men," *JAAPP Physiol*, 86, (1999): 29-39.

Carnitine. *The Medical Letter*, 28, (1986): 88.

Carroll, C. *Drugs In Modern Society, 5th ed.*, Boston, McGraw Hill, 2000.

Carter, J., and N. Rudd. "Disordered Eating Assessment For College Student-Athletes," *Women Sport Phy. Act. J.* 14, (2005): 62-72.

Cermak, T. and A. Rosenfield. Therapeutic Considerations With Adult Children of Alcoholics, in *Children of Alcoholics*, edited by M. Bean-Bayog and B. Stimmel. New York: Haworth Press, 1987.

Chernoff, G. "New Research On Pot Released," *U.S. Journal*, 15, (1991): 11.

Christen, A. "The Four Most Common Alterations of the Teeth, Periodontium and Oral Soft Tissues Absorbed In Smokeless Tobacco Users: A Literature Review," *J Indiana Dental Association*, 64, (1985): 15-18.

Cigars: Health Effects and Trends. *Smoking and Tobacco Control Monograph No. 9* Bethesda, MD: National Cancer Institute, February 1998. (NIH Publication No. 98-4302).

Cigar Smoking Among Teenagers – United States, Massachusetts, and New York, 1996. *MMWR Morb Mortal Wkly Rep 1997*; 46: 433-40.

Clark, N. *Nancy Clark's Sports Nutrition Guidebook*, 5th ed., Champaign, IL: Human Kinetics, 2014.

Cohen, S. *The Substance Abuse Problems*. New York, Haworth Press, 1981.

Committee On Substance Abuse Research and Education, *USOC Drug Control Program: Questions and Answers*, Colorado Springs US Olympic Committee, 1987.

Cowart, V. "Erythropoietin: A Dangerous New Form of Blood Doping?" *Physician Sportsmedicine*, 17, (1989): 115-118.

Cowart, V. "Human Growth Hormone the Latest Ergogenic Aid?" *Physician Sportsmedicine*, 16, 3, (March 1988): 175.

Cowart, V. "Some Predict Increased Steroid Use In Sports Despite Drug Testing Crackdown On Suppliers," *JAMA*, 257, (1987): 3025-3026.

Curran, J., Lawrence, D., Jaffe, H., et al. "Acquired Immune-Deficiency Syndrome (AIDS) Associated With Transfusion," *N Engl J Med*, 310, (1984): 69-75.

Davies, O. "The DMSO War," *Continuum*, (1989): 39.

Davis, E., Loiacono, R., and R. Summers. "The Rush to Adrenaline: Drugs in Sport Acting on The Beta-Adrenergic System," *Br J Pharmacol*, 154, (2008): 584-597.

Department of Agriculture, Tobacco Situation and Outlook Report. *Economic Research Service Series TBS-239*. Washington, DC: Government Printing Office, September 1997.

"Depression: What You Need To Know," *Mental Health America*, Retrieved: 9/24/07, from: http://www.mentalhealthamerica.net/go/information/get-info/depression-what-you-need-to-know.

Dezelsky, T., Toohey, J., and R., Shaw. "Non-Medical Drug Use Behavior at First United States Universities: A 15 Year Study," *Bull Narc*. 37, 2-3, (1985): 49-53.

Dipalma, J. "L-Carnitine: Its Therapeutic Potential," *American Family Physician*, 34, (1986): 127.

Dover, A. and W. Shultz. "Transfusion-Induced Malaria," *Transfusion*, 11, (1971): 353-357.

Drowns-Bangert, R. "The Effects of School Based Substance Abuse Education: A Meta-Analysis," *J Drug Education*, 18, 3, (1988): 243-264.

Duffy, D. and R. Conlee. "Effects of Phosphate Loading On Leg Power and High Intensity Treadmill Exercise," *Med Sci Sports Exerc*, 18, (1986): 674-677.

Duncan, D. and R. Gold. *Drugs and the Whole Person*. New York, John Wiley and Sons, 1982.

Eissenberg, T., Ward, K., Smith-Simone, S, et al. "Waterpipe Tobacco Smoking On a U.S. College Campus: Prevalence and Correlates," *J Adolesc Health*, 42, (2008): 526-529.

Ekblom, B., Wilson, G., and P. Astrand. "Cental Circulation During Exercise After Venesection and Reinfusion of Red Blood Cells," *J App Physiol*, 40, (1976): 379-383.

Ellis, D. "Pulling the Plug On Energy Drinks," *USA Hockey Magazine*, October, 2006.

Ernster, V., Grady, D., Greene, J., et al. "Smokeless Tobacco Use and Health Effects Among Baseball Player," *JAMA*, 264, 2, (1990): 218-224.

Eschbach, J., Egrie, J., Downing, M., et al. "Correction of the Anemia of End-Stage Renal Disease With Recombinant Human Erythropoietin. Results of a Combined Phase 1 and 2 Clinical Trial," *N Engl J Med*, 316, (1987): 73-78.

"FDA Bans Steroid," *The Boston Globe*, 29 October 2003.

Fields, R. *Drugs In Perspective: Causes, Assessment, Family, Prevention, Intervention, and Treatment, 8th ed.*, Boston, McGraw Hill, 2013.

Fink, H. and A. Mikesky. *Practical Applications in Sports Nutrition*, 4th ed., Burlington, MA: Jones and Bartlett Learning.

Gall, G. Marty, D. and D. Giel. "Who Tests Which Athletes For What Drugs?" *Physician and Sportsmedicine*, 16, 2, (February, 1988): 155-179.

"Gene Doping," *WADA*, 1 (2005): 2-6.

Gerlinger, K., Petermann, T. and A. Sauter. *Gene Doping*, Berlin, Germany, Office of Technology Assessment at The German Bundestag, 2008.

Gledhill, N. "Blood Doping and RElated Issues: A Brief Review," *Med Sci Sports Exerc*, 14, (1982): 183-189.

Glover, E., Schroeder, K., Henningfield, J., et al. "An Interpretative Review of Smokeless Tobacco Research In the United States," *J Drug Ed*, 19, 1, (1989): 1-19.

Goldberg, R. *Drugs Across the Spectrum, 6th ed.*, Belmont, CA, Thomson Wadsworth, 2010.

Goldman, B., Bush, P., and R. Klatz. *Death In the Locker Room: Steroids and Sports*. South Bend, Indiana, Icarus Press, 1984.

Goldman, B. and R. Klatz. *The E Factor*. New York, William Morrow and Co., 1988.

Grady, G. and T. Chalmers. "Risk of Post-Transfusion Viral Hepatitis," *N Engl J Med*, (1964): 271-337.

Greenwalt, T. (ed). *General Principles of Blood Transfusion*. Chicago, American Medical Association, 1977.

Groves, D. "Studies: Bicarbonate Doping Has No Benefits," *Physician Sportmedicine*, 15, (1987): 51.

Han, H., and Mitch, W. "Targeting The Myostatin Signalling Pathway to Treat Muscle Wasting Diseases," *Current Opinion in Supportive and Palliative Care*, 5 (2011): 334-341.

Hanson, G., P. Venturelli, and A. Fleckenstein. *Drugs and Society, 10th ed*. Boston. Jones & Bartlett Publishers 2009.

Hatfield, F. *Bodybuilding a Scientific Approach*. Chicago, Contemporary Books, 1984.

Haupt, H. and G. Rovere. "Anabolic Steroids: A Review of the Literature," *Am J Sports Med*. 12, (1984): 469-484.

Hemila, H. "Vitamin C Supplementation and Common Cold Symptoms: Factors Affecting the Magnitude of the Benefit," *Med Hypothesis*., 52, (1999): 171-178.

Herer, J. *Hemp & Marijuana Conspiracy: The Emperor Wears No Clothes*. Van Nuys, CA, Queen of Clubs Publishing, 1990.

Hermansen, L. and J. Medbo. "The Relative Significance of Aerobic and Anaerobic Processes During Maximal Exercise of Short Duration," *Med Sports Sci*, 17, (1984): 56.

"Hold That Hormone," *Modern Maturity*, March-April, 2000.

Hollister, L. "Health Aspects of Cannabis," *Pharmacological Reviews*. 38, (1986): 39-42.

Hong-Brown, I., Frost, R., and C. Lang. "Alcohol Impairs Protein Synthesis and Degradation in Cultured Skeletal Muscle Cells," *Alcohol Clin Ex Res*, 25, (2001), 1373-1382.

"How To Quit Smoking Using Nicoderm," Marion Merrell Dow Inc., 1991.

Hurley, B., Seals, D. Hagberg, J., et al. "High-Density-Lipoprotein Cholesterol In Bodybuilders and Powerlifters, Negative Effects of Androgen Use," *JAMA*. 252, (1984): 507-513.

Institute of Medicine. *Dietary Reference Intakes For Energy, Carbohydrate, Fiber, Fat, Fatty Acids, Cholesterol, Protein and Amino Acids*. Food and Nutrition Board. Washington, DC: National Academies Press, 2002.

Iribarren, C., Tekawa, I., Disney, S., et al. "Effects of Cigar Smoking On Rise of Cardiovascular Disease, Chronic Obstructive Pulmonary Disease, and Cancer In Men," *N. Engl. J. Med.*, 340, (1999): 1773-1779.

Jain, S. "Effect of Phosphate Supplementation On Oxygen Delivery at High Altitude," *Int J Biometor*, 31, (1987): 249.

Jenkins, M.A., "Creatin Supplementation In Athletics: Review," *Sports Med Web*, 1998 Http://riceinfo.rice.edu/~jenky/sports/creatine.html.

Jha P, Ramasundarahettige C, Landsman V, et al. "21st Century Hazards of Smoking and Benefits of Cessation in the United States," *New England Journal of Medicine*, 50, (2013): 368:341.

Johnston, L. "Illicit Drug Use, Drinking and Smoking: National Survey Results From America's High School Students, College Students and Young Adults Populations, 1975-1991," Rockville, MD, *NIDA*, 1991.

Joyce, S., Sabapathy, S., Bulmer, A., "The Effect of Prior Eccentric Exercies on Heavy-Intensity Cycling: The Role of Gender and Oral Contraceptives," *European J Applied Physiology*, 114, (2014): 995-1003.

Karch, S. Karch's *Pathology of Drug Abuse*, 4th ed. Taylor and Frances, 2008.

King, D., Sharp, P., Vukovich, M., et al. "Effects of Oral Androstenedione On Serum Testosterone and Adaptations to Resistance Training In Young Men," *JAMA*, 281, (1999): 2020-2028.

Klein, L., Berger, R. and J. Kearney. "The Effect of Bicarbonate Ingestion On Upper Body Power In Trained Athletes, " *Med Sci Sports Exerc*, 19, (Suppl. 1987): S67

Kuhn, C., Swartzwelder, S. and W. Wilson. *Pumped*. New York, W.W. Norton & Company, 2000.

Kumar, R., Negi, P., Singh, B. et al. "Cordyceps Sinensis Promotes Exercise Endurance Capacity of Rats By Activating Skeletal Muscle Metabolic Regulators," *J. Ethnopharmacology*, 136, (2011): 260-266.

Kumar, V., Atherton, P., Smith, K. et al. "Human Muscle Protein Synthesis and Breakdown During and After Exercise," *J Appl Physiol*, 106, (1985), 2009, 2026-2039.

Leit, R., Gray, J. and H. Pope. "The Media's Representation of the Ideal Male Body: A Cause For Muscle Dysmorphia?" *Inter. J. Eating Disorders*. 31, (2001): 334-338.

Leone, J., Sedory, E., and K. Gray. "Recognition and Treatment of Muscle Dysmorphia and Related Body Image Disorders." *J. Athletic Training*. 40, (2005): 352-359.

"Licorice In Chewing Tobacco Linked to High Blood Pressure," *Morning Sun*, 28, January, 1988.

Long, J. *The Essential Guide to Prescription Drugs*. New York, Harper and Row Publisher, 1982.

Mahesh, V., and R. Greenblatt. "The In-Vivo Conversion of Dhydroprendrosterone and Androstendedione to Testosterone In the Human," *ACTA Endocrinol*. 41, (1962): 400-406.

Martinasek, M., McDermott, R., and Martini, L. "Waterpipe (Hookah) Use Among Youth," *Curr Probl Pediatr Adolesc Health Care*, 41, (2011): 37-51.

Masouredis, S. "Preservation and Clinical Use of Erythrocytes and Whole Blood," in Williams, W., Beutler, E., Erslev, A., et al. (eds). Hematology, 2nd ed., New York, McGraw-Hill Inc., 1977.

Mayer, G., Thum, J., Cada, E., et al."Working Capacity is Increased Following Recombinant Human Erythropoietin Treatment," *Kidney Int*, 34, (1988): 525-528.

McGrath, M. and R. Penny. "Paraproteinuria: Blood Hyperviscosity and Clinical Manifestations," *J Clin Invest*, 58, (1976): 1155-1162.

Michigan Department of Community Health, Guidance Document Selecting, Planning, and Implementing Evidence-Based Interventions For the Prevention of Substance Use Disorders, January 2012.

Mindell, E. *Earl Mindell's Vitamin Bible*. New York, Warner Books, 1979.

Minelli, M. "Absinthe Comeback?" *EAP Digest*, 19, (March/April, 1999): 13.

Minelli, M. "Anabolic Steroids: Drug of the "80's," *Michigan School Health Association: Update, 2*, April/May, 1989.

Minelli, M. "Group Aims to Show Benefits of Using Marijuana," *U. S. Journal*, 15, 2, (December 1991): 5.

Minelli, M., Davenport, R., Debruin, R., and S. Campbell. "The Status of EAPS In Higher Education." *EAP Digest*, 18, (September/October, 1998): 27-28.

Minelli, M., Gay, J. and R. Rapaport. "Drug Education and Exploration Program: A Review," *New Jersey J Professional Counseling*, 51, 1/2, (1988): 20-23.

Minelli, M. and S. Smith. "Performance Enhancing Drugs: The Ethical Dilemma," *Interscholastic Athletic Administration*, Winter, (2012): 4-6.

Minelli, M., Thompson, P. and R. Rapaport. "Anabolic-Androgenic Steroid Use-Abuse (In Males) Progression Chart." *Addiction & Recovery*, (September/October, 1991): 14-16.

Mottram, D. and N. Chester. *Drugs In Sports*, 6th ed., London, Routledge, 2015.

Murphree, H. "Some Possible Origins of Alcoholism," Chapter 4 in *Alcohol and Alcohol Problems: New Thinking and New Directions*, Filstead, W., Rossi, J. and M. Keller, (ed). Cambridge, Mass, Ballinger, (1976): 140-141.

Murray, T. "The Ethics of Drugs In Sports," in Strauss, R. (ed): *Drugs and Performance In Sports*. Philadelphia, W. B. Saunder Co., 1987.

National Association For Sport & Physical Education. "Guidelines for Establishing a Policy On Substance Abuse By Student-Athletes," 1989.

National Dairy Council. *Food Power: A Coach's Guide to Improving Performance*. Rosemont, IL., 1983.

National Institute On Drug Abuse, "Bath Salts-Emerging and Dangerous Products," February 2011, http://www.drugabuse.gov/about-nida/directors-page/messages. director/2011/02bath-salts-emerging-dangerous-products.

National Institute On Drug Abuse, "Drugs, Brains, and Behavior: The Science of Addiction," August 2010, http://www.drugabuse.gov/publications-addiction/drugs-brain.

National Institute On Drug Abuse, "Drug Facts: Spice (Synthetic Marijuana)," May 2012, http://www.drugabuse.gov/publications/drugfacts/spice-synthetic-marijuana.

National Institute On Drug Abuse, "Important Treatment Advances For Addiction to Heroin and Other Opiates," October 2012, http://www.drugabuse.gov/about-nida/directors-page/messages-director/2010/10important-treatment-advances-addiction-to-heroin-other-opiates.

NCAA. (2004, May 12). *Executive Summary For the National Study On Collegiate Sports Wagering and Associated Health Risks*. Retrieved 5/26/04, from: http://www.ncaa.org/gambling/2003nationalstudy/slideshow.

NCAA National Study of Substance Abuse Use habits of College Student-Athletes, Final Report, July 2014.

1989/90 NCAA Drug Education Testing Programs, National Collegiate Athletic Association, Mission, Kansas, July 1989.

"New Over-the-Counter Steroids Anger U.S. Officials," *Washington Post*, 6 December 2002.

Newton, D. Steroids and Doping in Sports. Santa Barbara, California, ABC-CLIO, 2014.

Nichols, K. "The Other Performance-Enhancing Drugs." *The Chronicle of Higher Education*, L1 (17 December 2004): A11.

"NIDA Launches First Large-Scale National Study to Treat Addiction to Prescription Pain Medications," *NIH News*, Retrieved: 3/9/07 from: http//www.nih.gov/news/pr/mar2007/nida-076.htm.

Olrich, T. and M. Ewing. "Life On Steroids: Bodybuilders Describe Their Perceptions of the Anabolic-Androgenic Steroid Use Period," *Sport Psychologist*. 13 (1999): 299-312.

O'Malley, P. and L. Johnston. "Drugs and Driving by American High School Seniors, 2001-2006," *J. of Studies on Alcohol and Drugs*. 68 (2007): 834-842.

Pace, N., Lozner, E., Consolazio, W., et al. "The Increase In Hypoxia Tolerance of Normal Men Accompanying the Polycythemia Induced By Transfusion of Erythrocytes," *Am J Physiol*, 148, (1947): 152-163.

"Painkiller Use Skyrockets," *The Morning Sun*, 21 August 2007.

PDR for Nonprescription Drugs, 35th ed., Montvale, NJ. PDF Network, 2014.

Pesta, D., Angadi, S., Burtscher, M. et al. "The Effects of Caffeine, Nicotine, Ethanol, and Tetrahydrocannabinol on Exercise Performance," *Nutrition & Metabolism*, 10, (2013):71.

Pedersen, D., Lessard, S., Coffey, V., et al. "High Rates of Muscle Glycogen Resynthesis After Exhaustive Exercise When Carbohydrate is Coingested With Caffeine," *J App Physiology*, 105, (2008):7-13.

Peterson, R. "Marijuana and Health," in Peterson (ed). *Monograph 31*, National Institute of Drug Abuse, 1980.

Physician's Desk Reference. Oradell, NJ, Medical Economics Company Inc., 1988.

Pokrywka, A., Tszyrsznic, W., and D. Kwiatkowska. "Problems of the Use of Pseudoephedrine By Athletes," *Inter J of Sports Med*, 30, (2009):569-572.

Pope, H. Jr., Ionescu-Pioggia, M., and J. Cole. "Drug Use and Life-Style Among College Undergraduates, Nine Years Later," *Arch Gen Psychiatry*. 38, (1981): 588-591.

Pope, H. Jr., and D. Katz. "Affective and Psychotic Symptoms Associated With Anabolic Steroid Use," *Am J Psychiatry*. 145, (1988): 487-490.

"Pot Advocates to Tell Their Story at CMU Monday," *Saginaw News*, 5 April 1991.

Primack, A., Sidani, J., Agarwal, A. et al. "Prevalence of and Associations With Waterpipe Tobacco Smoking Among U.S. University Students," *Ann Behav Med*, 36, (2008):81-86.

"Pumped Up," *U. S. News & World Report*, 1 June 1992.

Reducing Tobacco Use: A Report of the Surgeon General (Atlanta: Centers For Disease Control and Prevention, 2000).

Robertson, R. Gilcher, R. Metz, K., et al. "Effect of Induced Erythrocythemia On Hypoxia Tolerance During Physical Exercise," *J App Physiol: Respirat Environ Exerc Physiol*, 53, (1982): 490-495.

Robertson, R. Gilcher, R. Metz, K., et al. "Hemoglobin Concentration and Aerobic Work Capacity In Women Following Induced Erythrocythemia," *J Appl Physiol: Respirat Environ Exerc Physiol*, 57, (1984): 568-575.

Robinson, K. and L. Verity. "Effects of Induced Alkalosis On Rowing Ergometer Performance During Repeat 1-Mile Work-Outs," *Med Sci Sports Exerc*, 19, (Suppl. 1987): S68.

Saal, D., Dong, Y., Bonci, A., and R. Malenka. "Drugs of Abuse and Stress Trigger a Common Synaptic Adaptation In Dopamine Neurons," *Neuron*, 37, (2003): 577-582.

Saugy, M., Avois, L., Saudan, C., et al. "Cannabis and Sport," *British J of Sports Medicine*, 40 (Suppl 1), (2006):i13-i15.

Schneider, A. and T. Friedman. *Gene Doping In Sports*. San Diego: Elsevier Academic Press, 2006.

Schroeder, D., Chen, M. Jr., and R. Kathy. "Smokeless Tobacco: The New Thing to Chew On." *Ohio Dental J*, 59, (1985): 11-14.

Scott, M. and K. Dedel. Clandestine Methamphetamine Labs (U.S. Department of Justice, August 2006).

"Secondhand Smoke and Disease," *Washington Post*, 25 March 1999.

Seligmann, J. and M. Hager. "Drug Test Creates a Doctor's Dilemma," *Newsweek*, Oct., 1989, 52.

Shaffer, H. and M. Hall. *Updating and Refining Meta-Analytic Prevalence Estimates of Disordered Gambling Behavior In the United States and Canada*. Boston, MA: Harvard Medical School, 2000.

Shannon, A. "Disordered Eating In Athletes," *Thesis – Central Michigan University*, August, 2007.

Sherman, W. "Metabolism of Sugars and Physical Performance," *Amer. J. Clin Nutri*, 62 (Suppl. 1995): S228-S241.

Shute, N. "Over the Limit," *U.S. News and World Report*, 142 (April 23, 2007): 60.

Sledhill, N. "Blood Doping and Related Issues: A Brief Review," *Med Sci Sports Exerc*. 14, (1982): 169-171.

Solberg, S. "Anabolic Steroids and Norwegian Weightlifters," *Br J Sports Med*. 3, (1982): 169-171.

"Sports Supplement Dangers," *Consumer Report*, June, 2001.

Spriet, L., Gledhill, N., Froese, A., et al. "Effect of Graded Erythrocythemia On Carbdiovascular and Metabolic Responses to Exercise," *J Appl Physiol*, 61, (1986): 1942-1948.

Stein, J., M. Leslie, and A. Nyamathi. "Relative Contributions of Parent Substance Use and Childhood Maltreatment to Chronic Homelessness", *Child Abuse and Neglect*, 26, (2002): 1011-1020.

Stern, E. *Prescription Drugs and Their Side Effects*. New York, Perigee Books, 1983.

Stewart, B. and A. Smith. rethinking Drug Use in Sport. New York, New York, Routledge Taylor and Francis Group, 2014.

Strass, R. (ed). *Drugs and Performance In Sports*. Philadelphia, W. B. Saunders Company, 1987.

Substance Abuse and Mental Health Services Administration, "The Effects of Alcohol On Women," Rockville, MD: *U. S. Department of Health and Human Services*, 2007.

"Supplement Use Widespread," *The Detroit News*, 15 August 2001.

Swenson, E., McKead, D. and D. Hough. "Anabolic Steroids: Statewide Survey of High School Football Coaches," *Med Sci Sports Exerc*, 20, (1988)(April Suppl): S24.

Tanner, L. "Teens E-Cigarette Use Linked With Later Smoking," *Morning Sun*, 24, August, 2015.

The 1987-88 NCAA Drug-Testing Program, Mission, KS, National Collegiate Athletic Association, 1987.

"The Continuing Coffee Controversy," *Medical Update*, 3, 11, May, 1990.

The Nation's Health, States Taking Action to Regulate E-Cigarettes, May/June 2015.

The Use of Anabolic-Androgenic Steroids In Sports, Revised Position Stand, Indianapolis, American College of Sports Medicine, 1984.

Thompson, J., Stone, J., Ginsberg, A., et al. "02 Transport During Exercise Following Blood Reinfusion," *J Appl Physiol: Respirat Environ Exerc Physiol*, 53, (1982): 1213-1219.

Thorn, G., Adams, R., Braunwald, E., et al. (eds). *Harrisons' Principles of Internal Medicine*, New York, McGraw-Hill Inc., 1977.

Todd, T. "The Steroid Predicament," *Sports Illustrated*, 1 August 1983, 63-78.

Toohey, J. "Nonmedical Drug Use Among Intercollegiate Athletes at Five American Universities," *Bull Narc*, 30, 3, (1978): 61-64.

Toohey, J. "Trends In Drug Use Behavior at Ten Arizona High Schools," *Ariz J Health Phys Ed Recreation*, 18, (1975): 6-8.

Toohey, J. and B. Cox. "Steroids and the Athlete," *Ariz J Health Phys Ed Recreation*, 14, (1971): 15-17.

Tucker, L. "Use of Smokeless Tobacco, Cigarette Smoking and Hypercholesterolemia," *Amer J Public Health*, 79, (1989): 1048-1050.

U.S. Department of Health, Education and Welfare. *The Smoking Digest*. 1977.

U.S. Department of Health and Human Services. *Results From the 2010 National Survey On Drug Use and Health: Summary of National Findings*.

U.S. Department of Health and Human Services. *The Health Consequences of Smoking—50 Years of Progress: A Report of the Surgeon General*. Atlanta: U.S. Department of Health and Human Services, Centers for Disease Control and Prevention, National Center for Chronic Disease Prevention and Health Promotion, Office on Smoking and Health, 2014.

Vaillant, G. *The Natural History of Alcoholism*. Cambridge, Mass, Harvard University Press, 1983.

Valeri, C. *Blood Banking and the Use of Frozen Blood Products*. CRC Press. 1976.

Walker, L., Bemben, M., Bemben, D., et al. "Chromium Picolinate Effects On Body Compostion and Muscular Performance In Wrestlers," *Med Sci Sports Exerc*, 30, (1998): 1730-1737.

Weil, A. *Spontaneous Healing*, New York, Fawcett Columbine Book, 1995.

Weil, A. "The Truth About the Fountain of Youth," *AARP*, May & June, 2007, 40.

Weil, A. and W. Rosen. *Chocolate to Morphine*. Boston, Houghton Mifflin Co., 1983.

Weiner, N. "Drugs That Inhibit Adrenergic Nerves and Block Adrenergic Receptors," in Gilman, A., et al. (eds). *Goodman and Gilman's the Pharmacological Basis of Therapeutics, ed. 7*, New York, MacMillan, 1985.

Weiss, R. "Take Two Puffs and Call Me In the Morning: Proponents of Marijuana's Medical Benefits Take Their Case to Court," *Science News*, 133, (1988): 122-123.

"White House Task Force On Drug Use In Sports Proceedings," 7 December 2000.

Wilcox, A. "Caffeine and Endurance Performance," *Gatorade Sports Science Institute*, 3, 26, May, 1990.

Wilhelm, M. "DMSO: No Proof of Miracles," *FDA Consumer*, (1980): 28-29.

Wilkes, K., Gledhill, N. and R. Smyth. "Effect of Acute Induced Metabolic Alkalosis On 800-M Racing Time," *Med Sci Sports Exerc*, 15, (1983): 277-280.

Williams, M. *Beyond Training: How Athletes Enhance Performance Legally and Illegally*. Champaign, IL., Leisure Press, 1989.

Williams, M. (ed). *Ergogenic Aids In Sport*. Champaign, IL, Human Kinetics Publisher, 1983.

Williams, M., Kreider, R. and J. Branch. *Creatine: The Power Supplement*. Champaign, IL, Human Kinetics Publishers, 1999.

Wilson, W. and E. Derse. *Doping in Elite Sport*. Champaign, Illinois, Human Kinetics Publishers, Inc., 2001.

Wisniewski, Jl, Mohl, G. and D. Shedroff. "Smokeless Tobacco Use By High School Baseball Players," *Health Education*, 21, 1, (1990): 10-15.

Witters, W. and P. Venturelli. *Drugs and Society, 2nd ed*. Boston, Jones and Bartlett Publishers, 1988.

Zimmerman, D. *The Essential Guide to Nonprescription Drugs*. New York, Harper and Row Publishers, 1983.

Index

A

B

C

D

E

F

G

O

P

Q

R

S

T

U

V

W

X

Y

Z

About the Author

Mark J. Minelli, MA, MPA, PhD., is currently a Professor at Central Michigan University (CMU) and Adjunct Professor at Capella University. In 1986 CMU became the first institution within the National Collegiate Athletic Association (NCAA) to mandate that all student-athletes take a drug education course and this manual is now used as the course syllabus. Dr. Minelli was previously the past Director of Substance Abuse Services, Inc., in Ludington, Michigan, and has extensive experience in both outpatient counseling and prevention services. He is nationally published in many health related journals including the *U.S. Journal of Drug and Alcohol Dependence, Addiction and Recovery, Journal of Physical Education, Recreation and Dance, Eta Sigma Gamma, Journal of College and Student Development, Topics in Clinical Nutrition*, and the *Journal of Alcohol and Drug Education*. His other books include: *Beyond Beer Goggles: Interactive Teaching Methods for Alcohol, Other Drugs and AIDS Prevention* (4th edition), *The Art of Living: Pathways to Personal Growth* (3rd edition), *Community Health Education: Settings, Roles, and Skills* (5th edition), and *Drugs of Abuse: A Quick Information Guide*. Dr. Minelli is an active consultant for films, school districts, national radio talk shows, newpapers, and businesses. He and his wife Debra have four children, seven grandchildren, and reside in Mt. Pleasant, Michigan.

Special Thanks to the Reviewers and Contributors

Reviewers

Ernest L. Minelli, Ed.D.
Professor & Vice Provost Emeritus
Central Michigan University

Ross J. Rapaport, Ph.D.
Professor of Counseling
Central Michigan University

Julie A Weisbrod, M.A.
Former Graduate Intern,
University Health Services
Central Michigan University

Contributors

James E. Hornak, Ed.D.
Past Department Chair,
Physical Education & Sport
Central Michigan University

Kenneth A. Dachman, Ph.D.
Author and Private Practitioner

Holly Whitehead
Consultant

Michael J. Maxwell
Graduate Research Assistant
Central Michigan University –
College of Medicine